# Drawing the Galaxy from the Light Side to the Dark Side with Melvin and Me

Written and Illustrated by
Shawn Durington

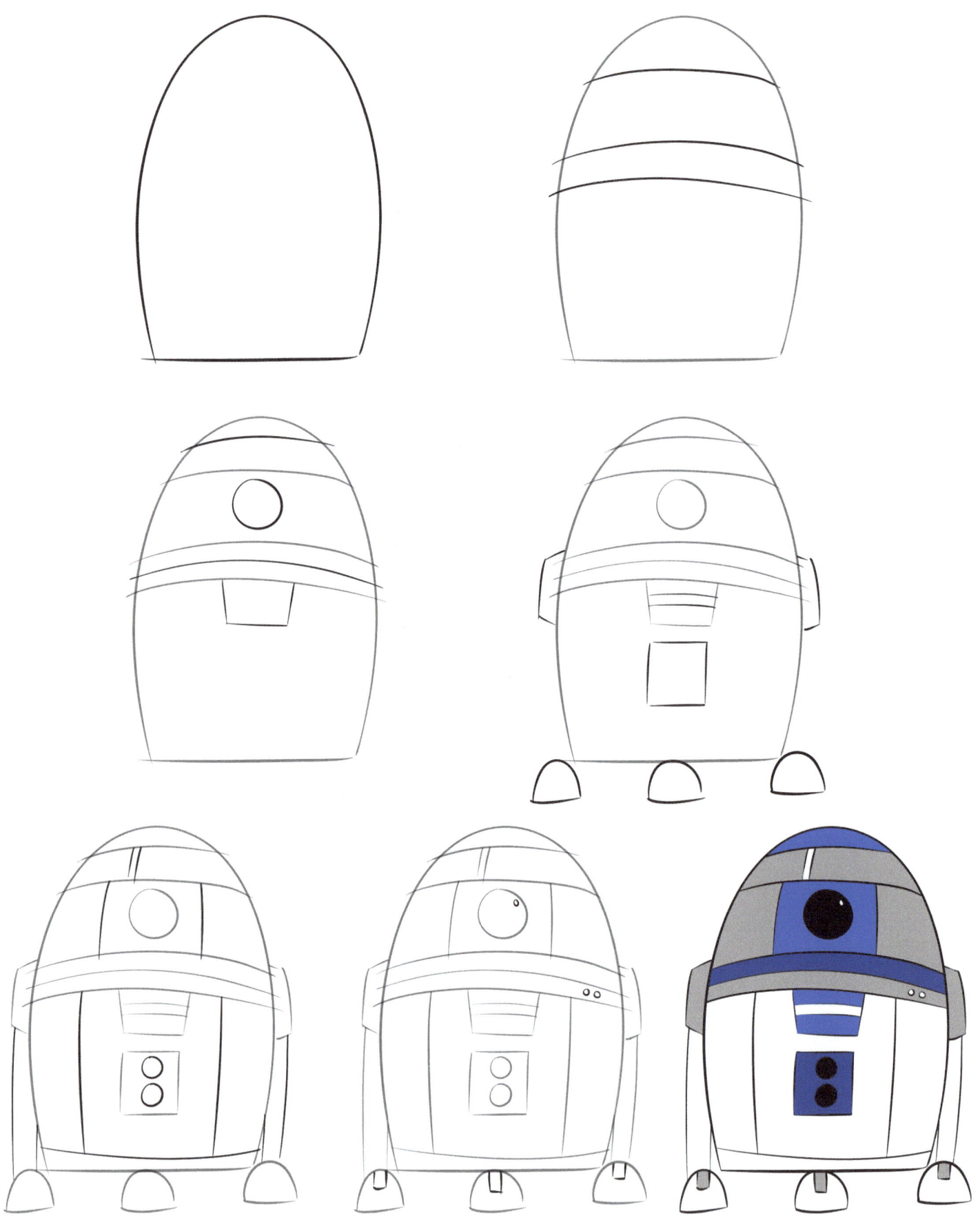

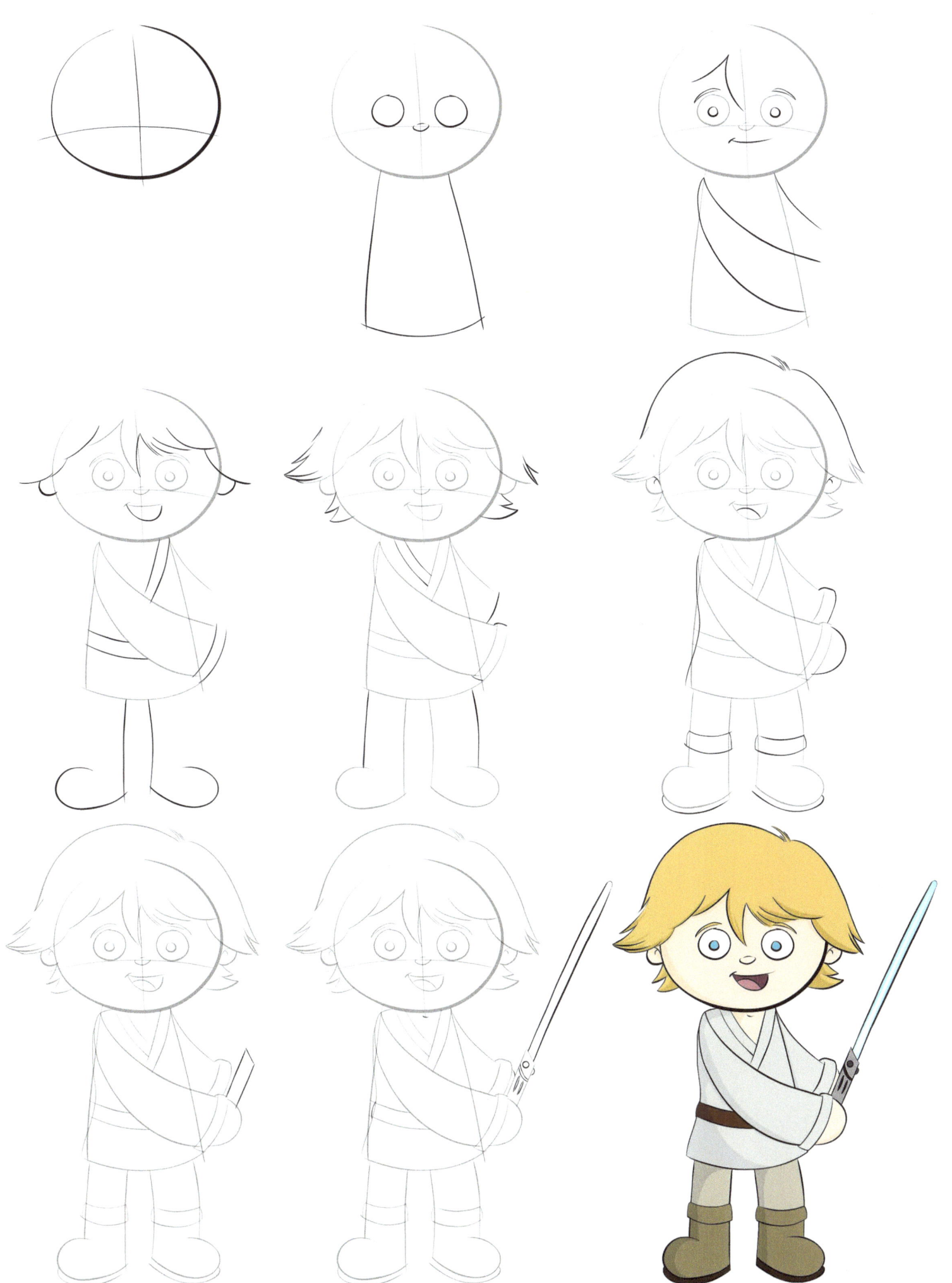

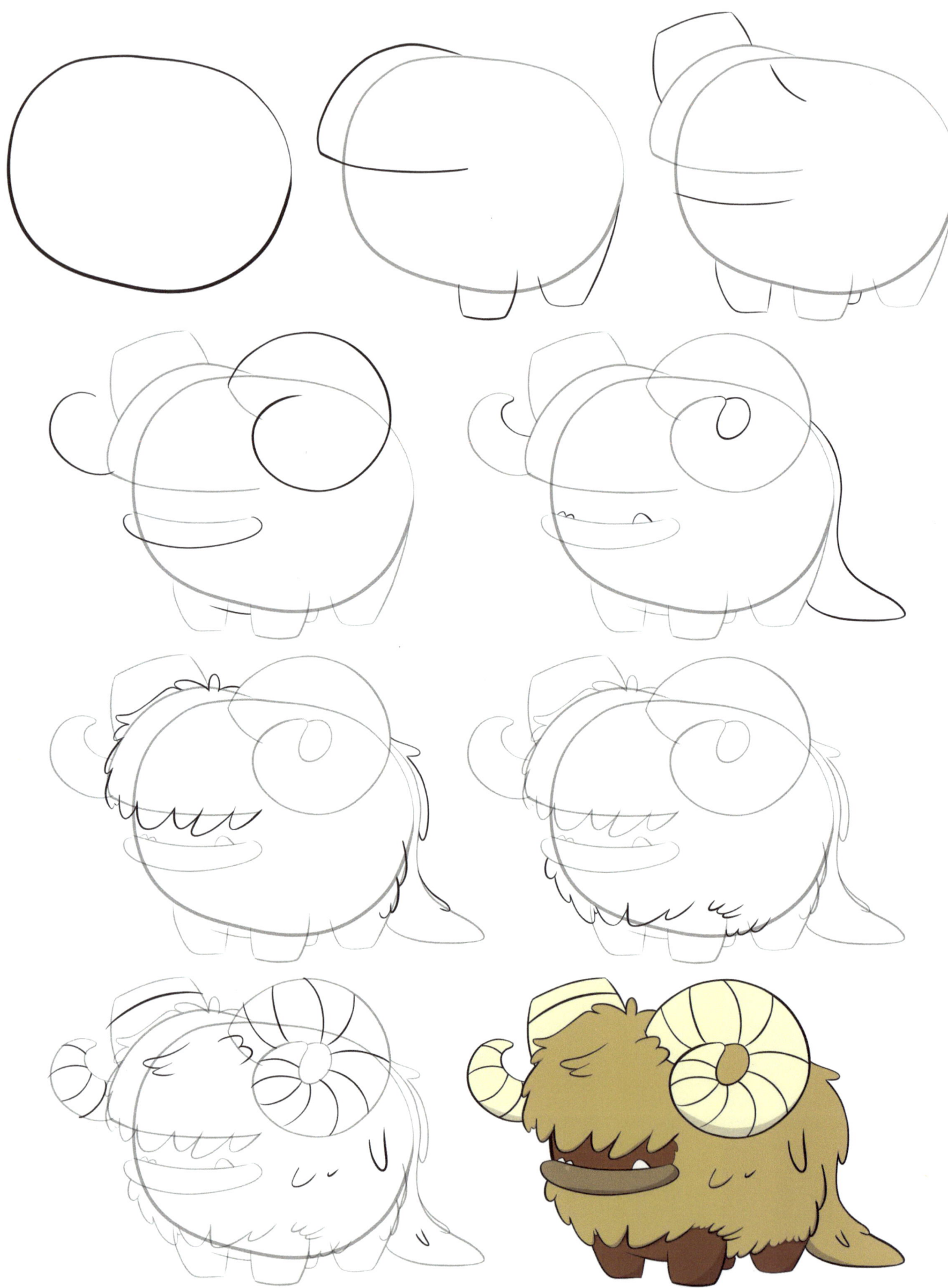

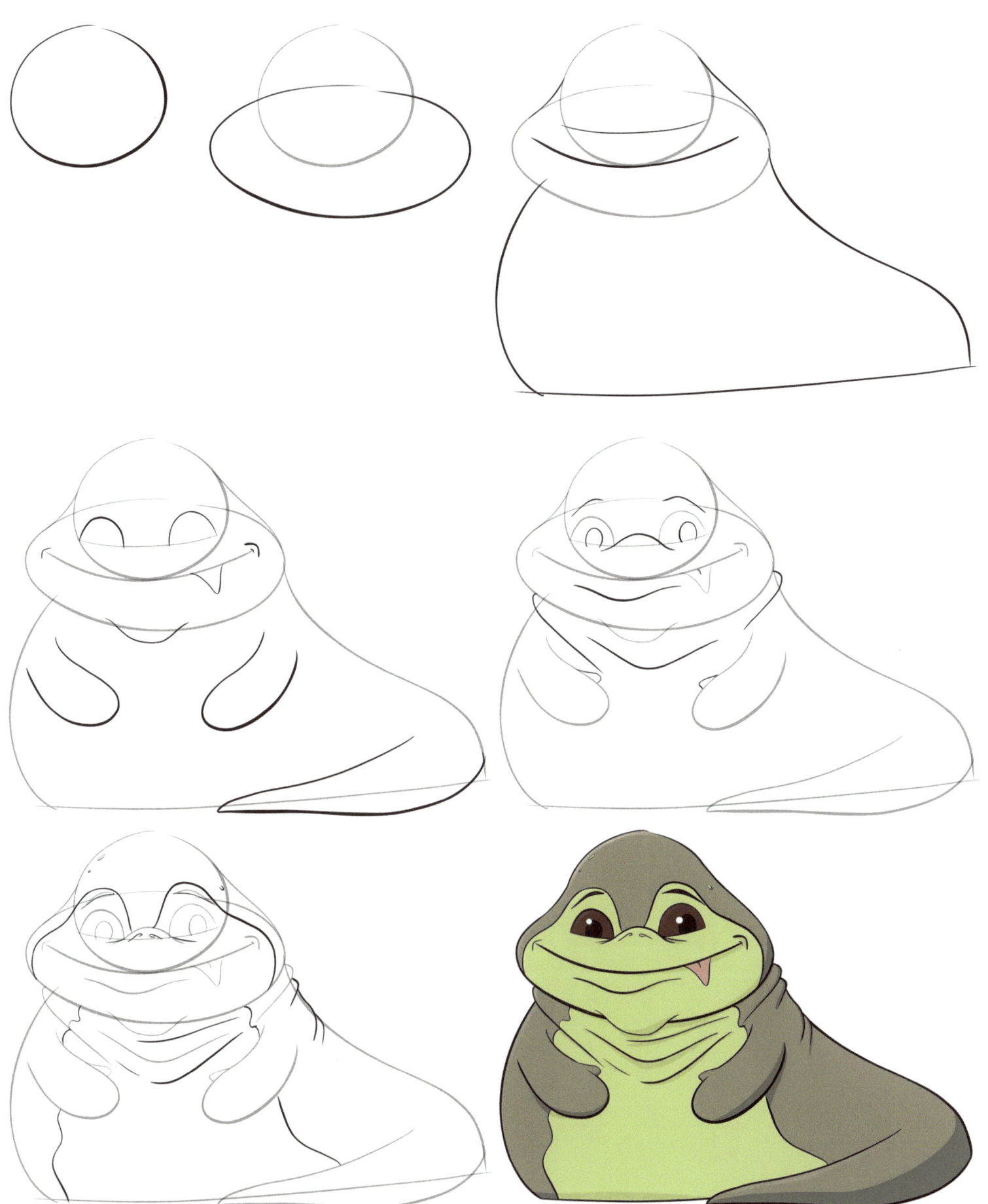

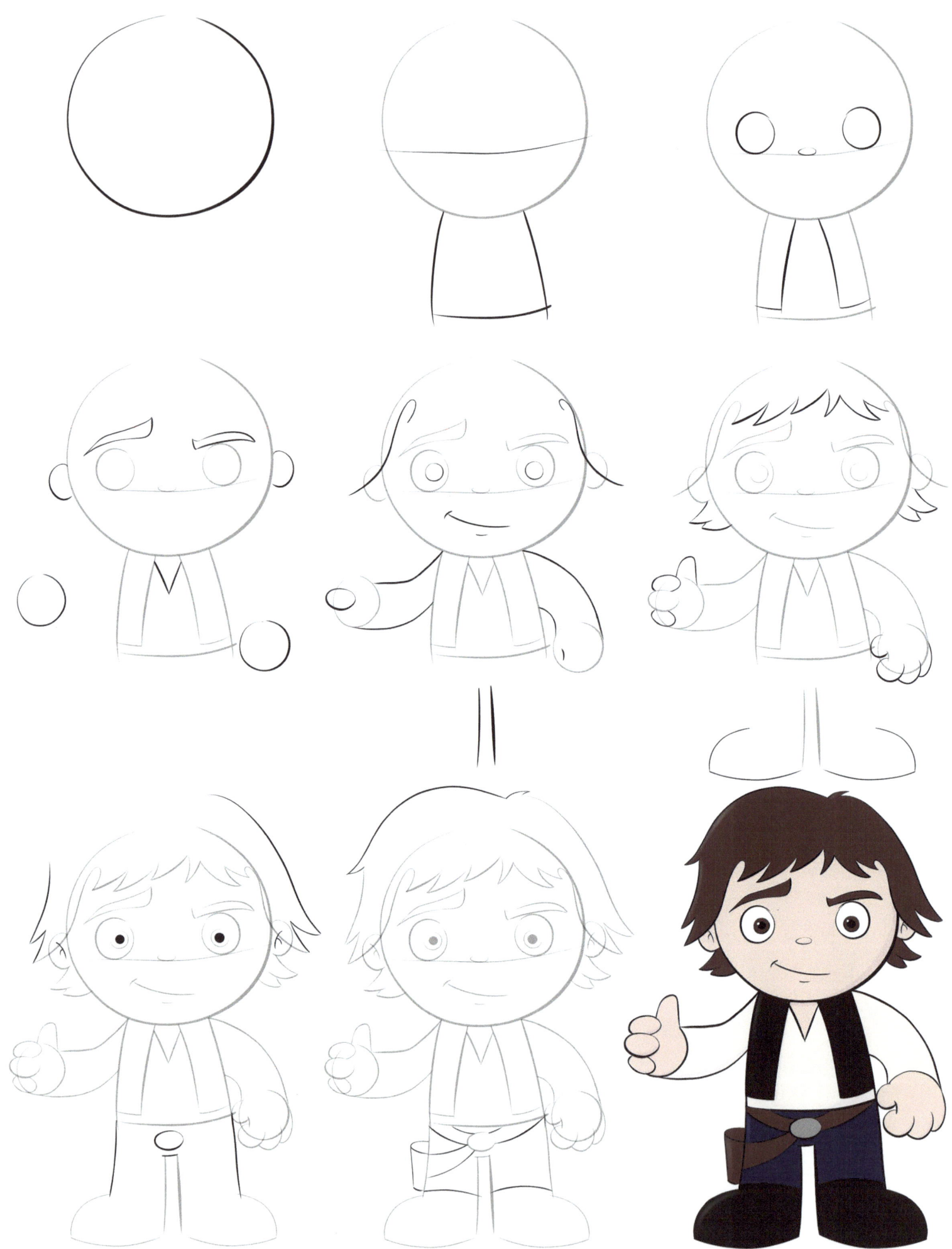

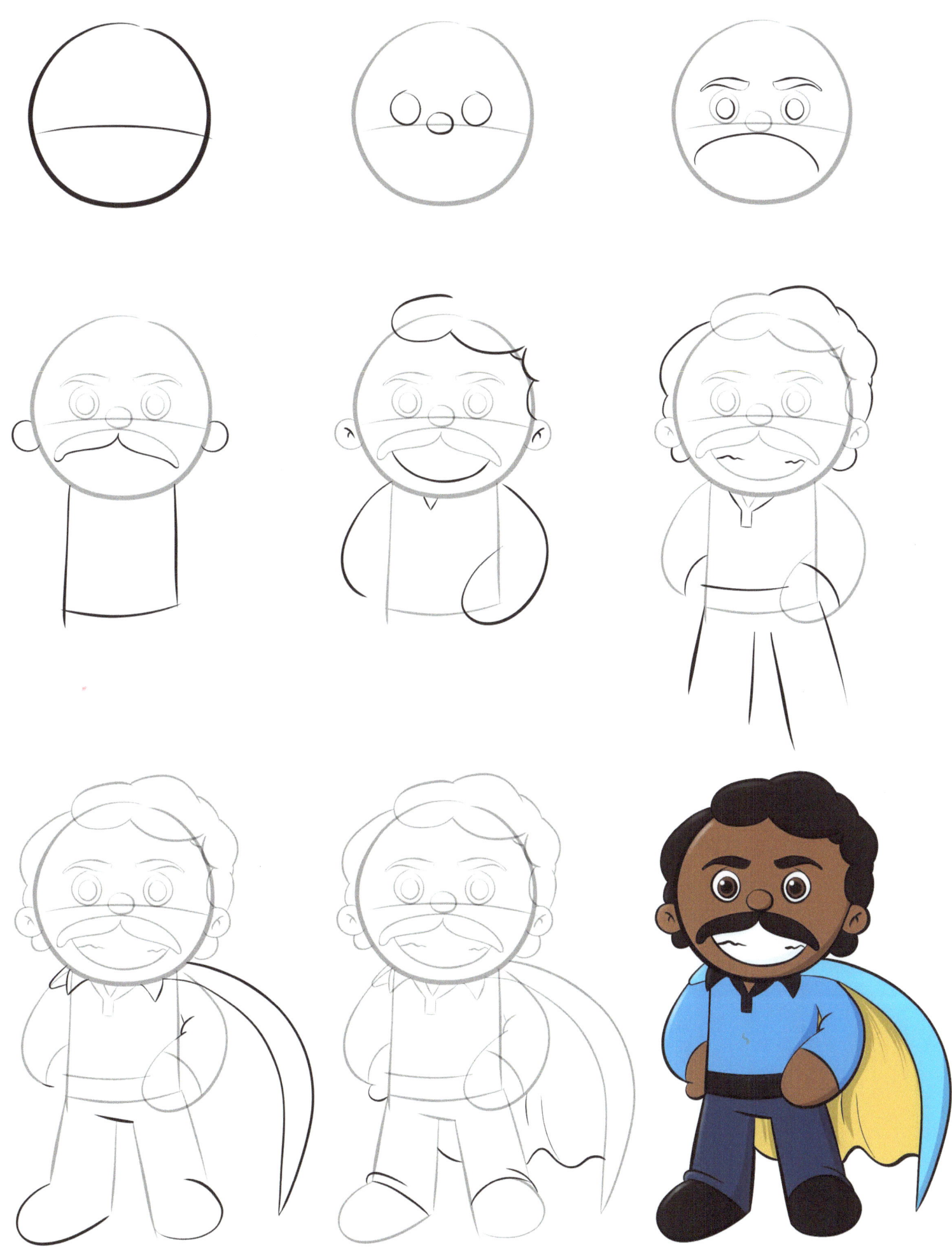

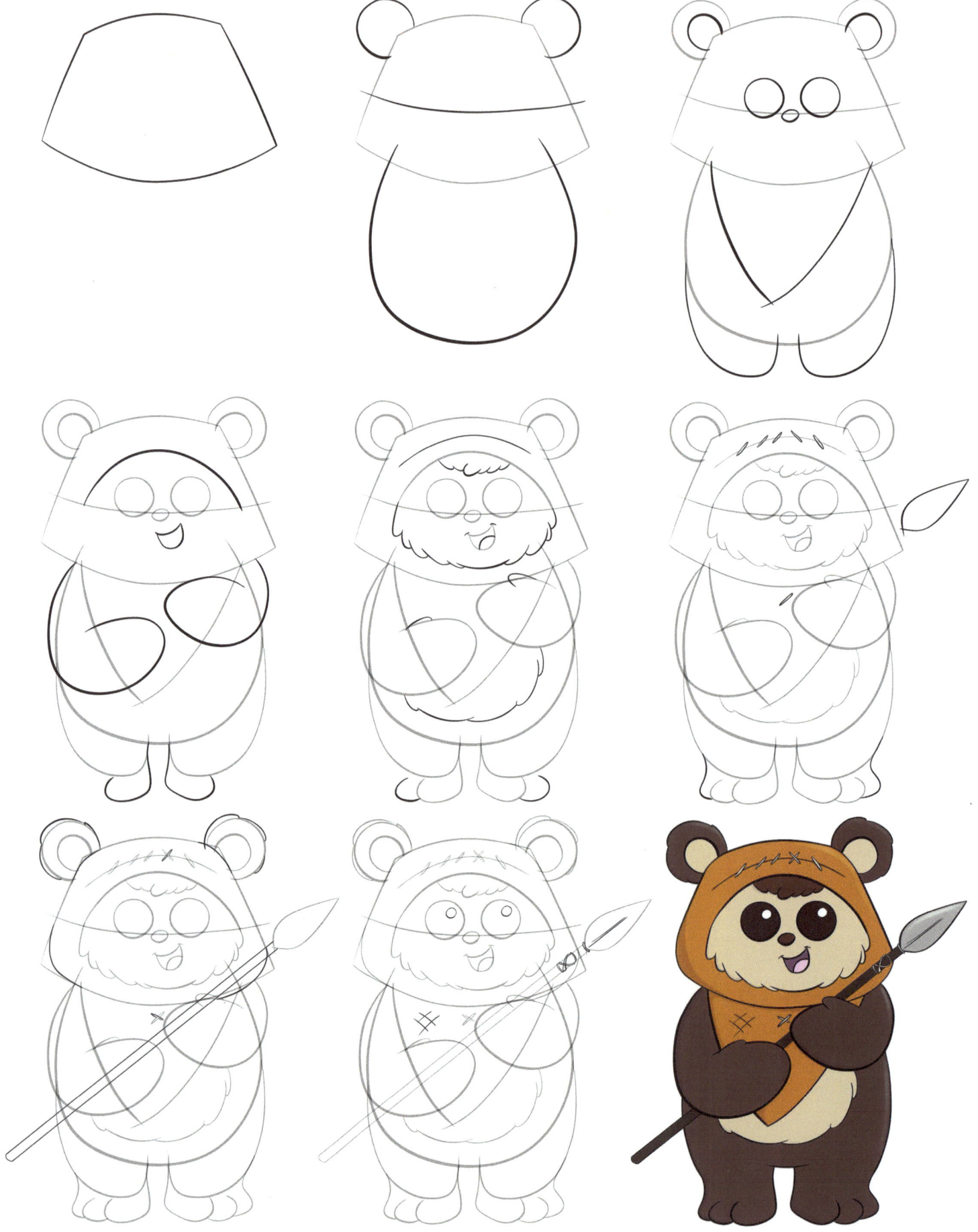

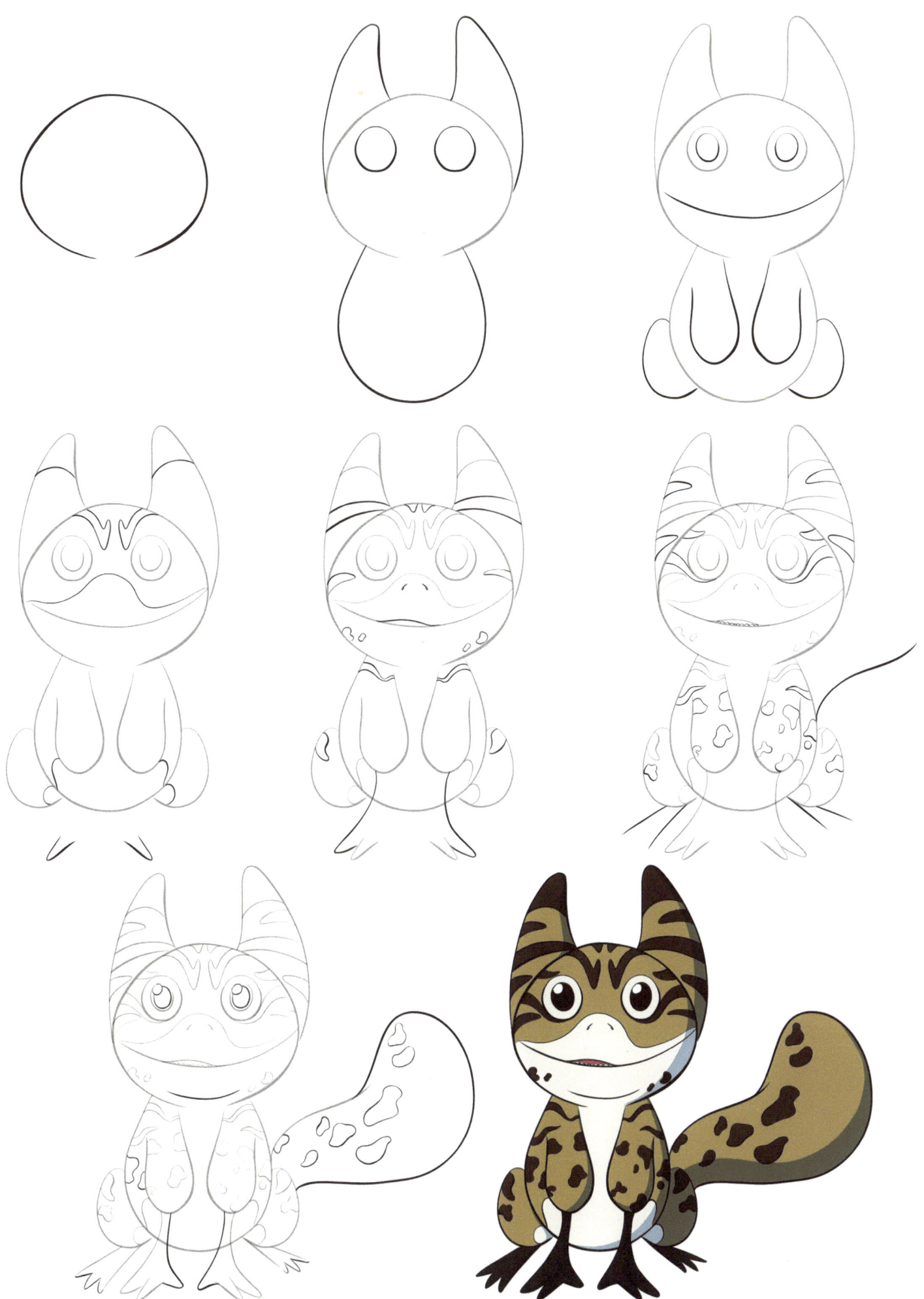

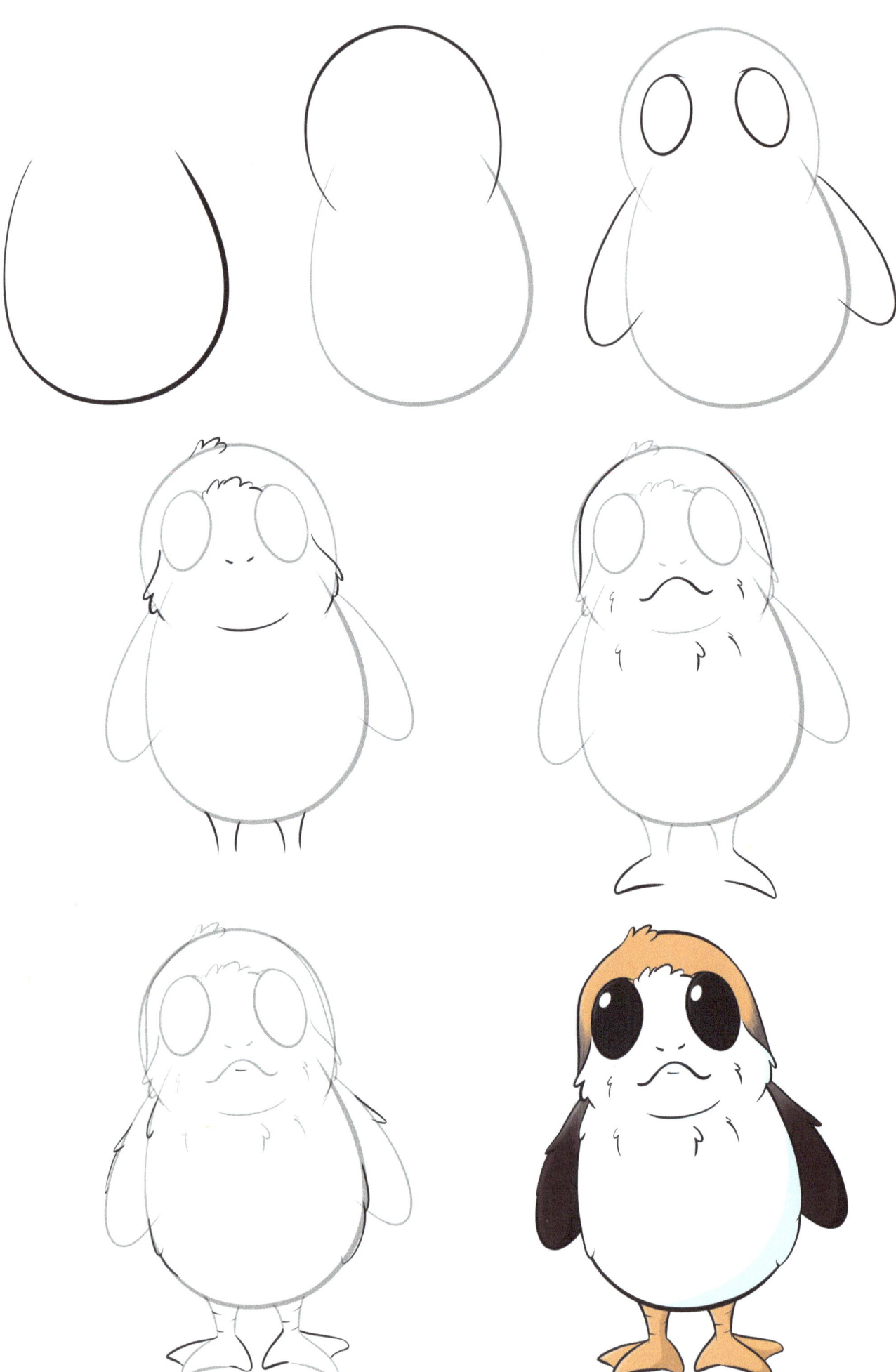

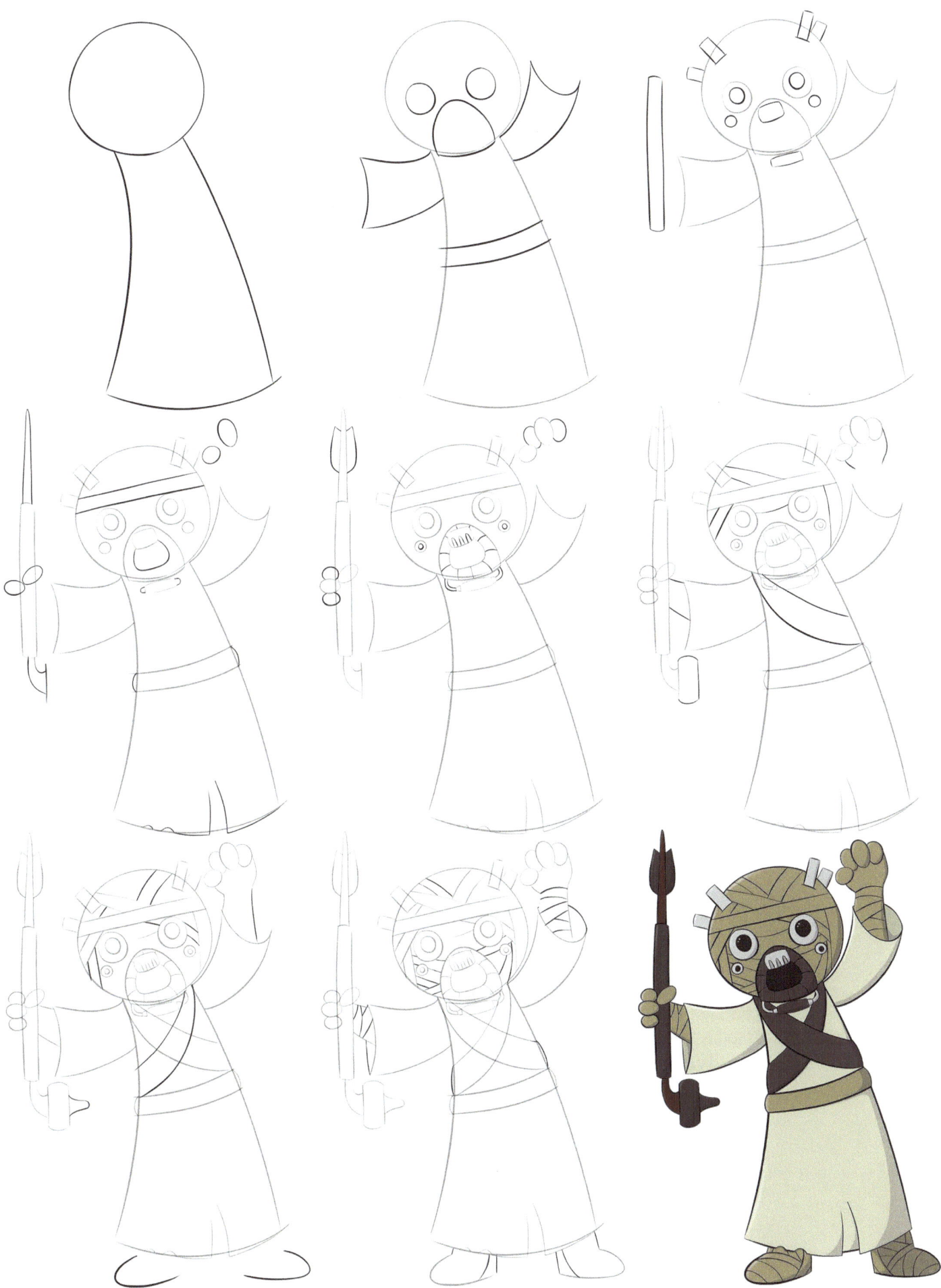

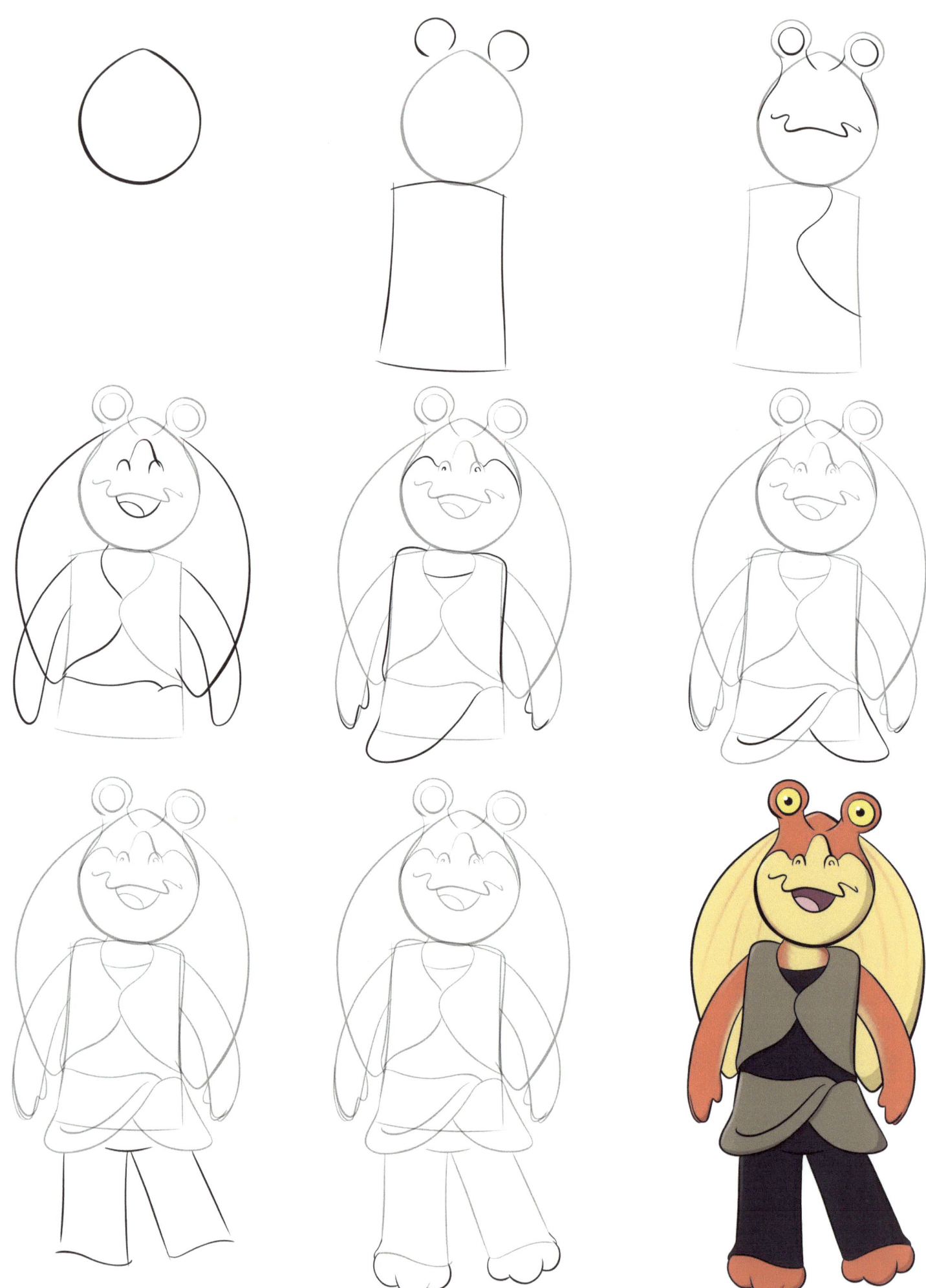

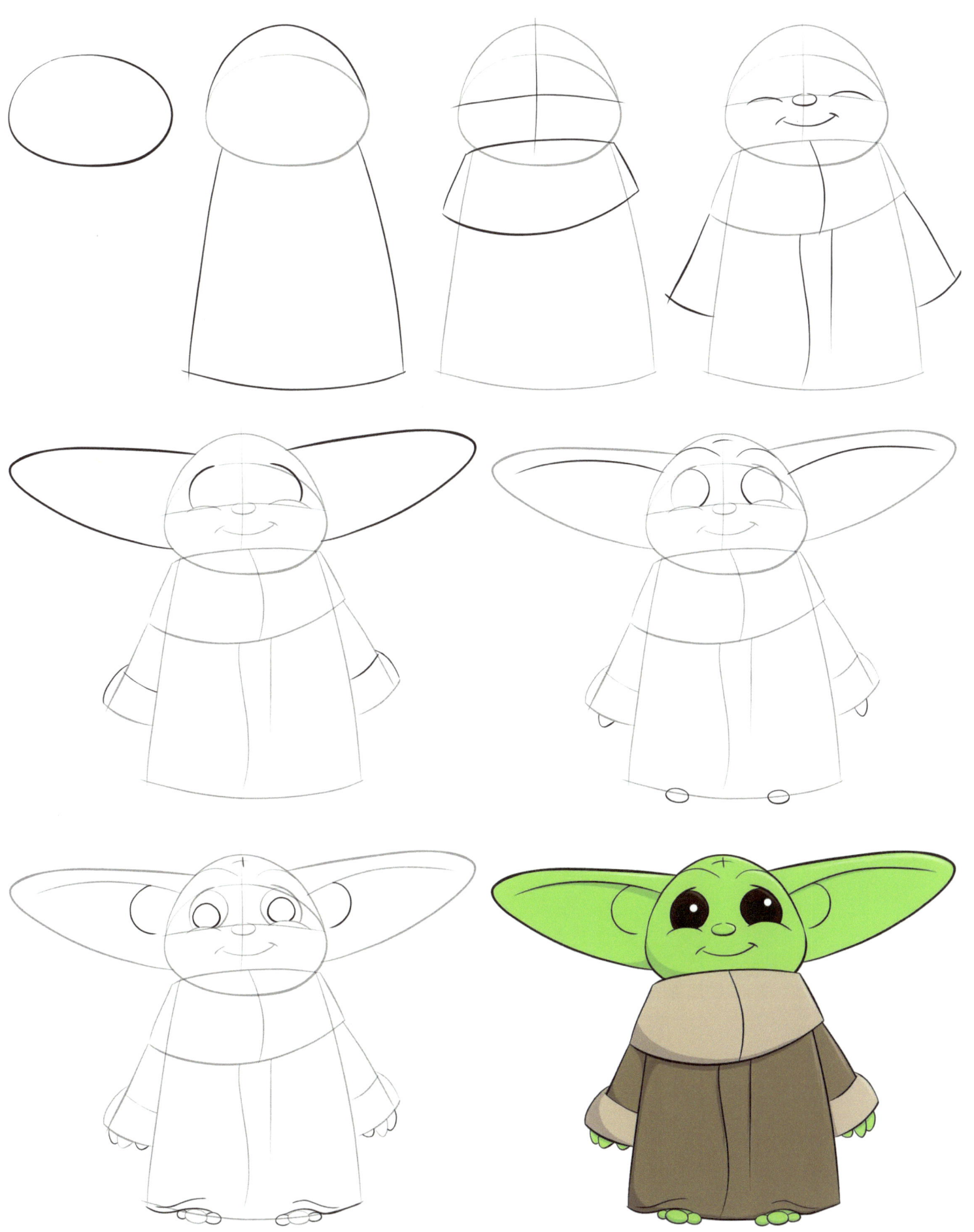

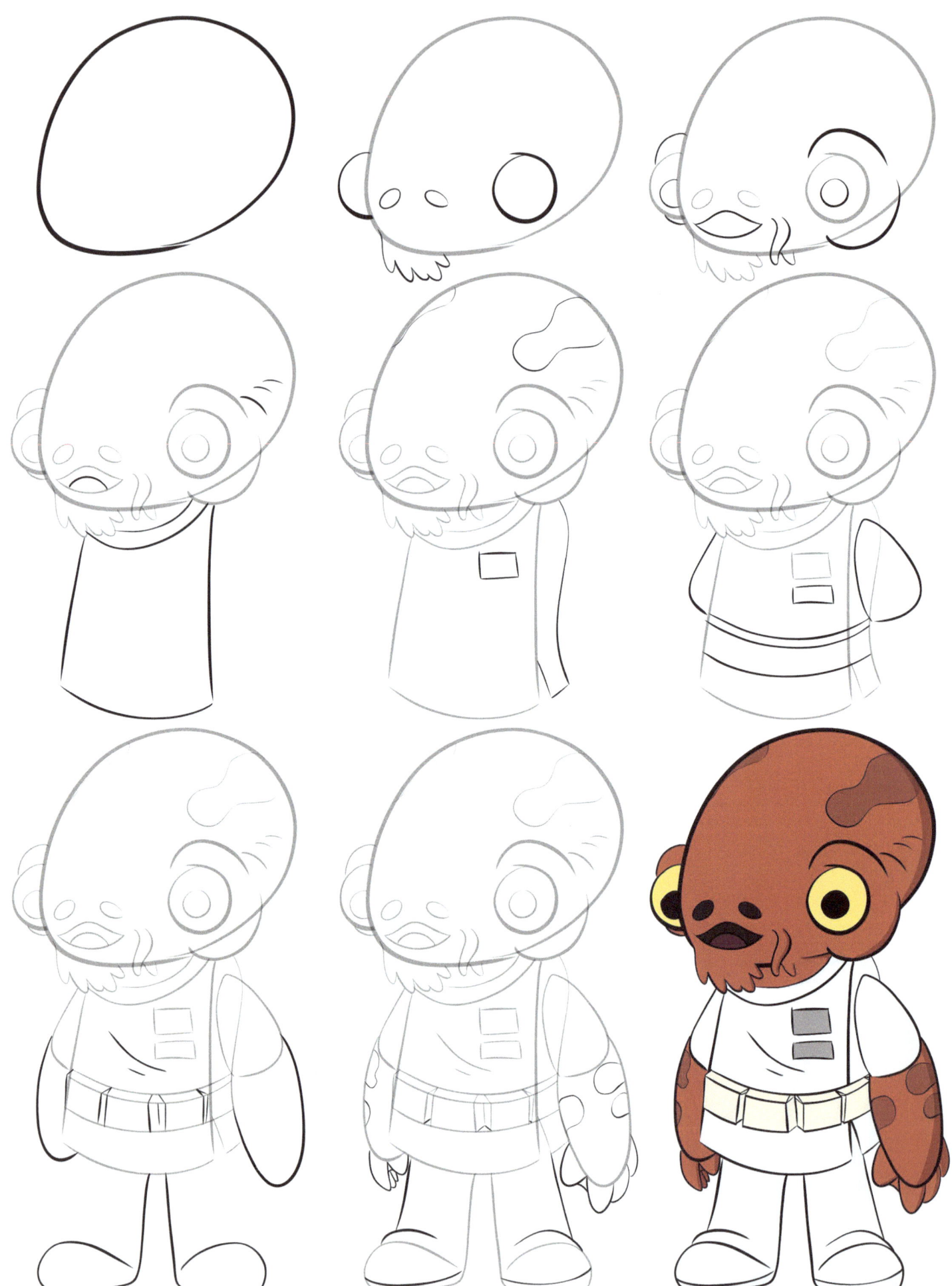

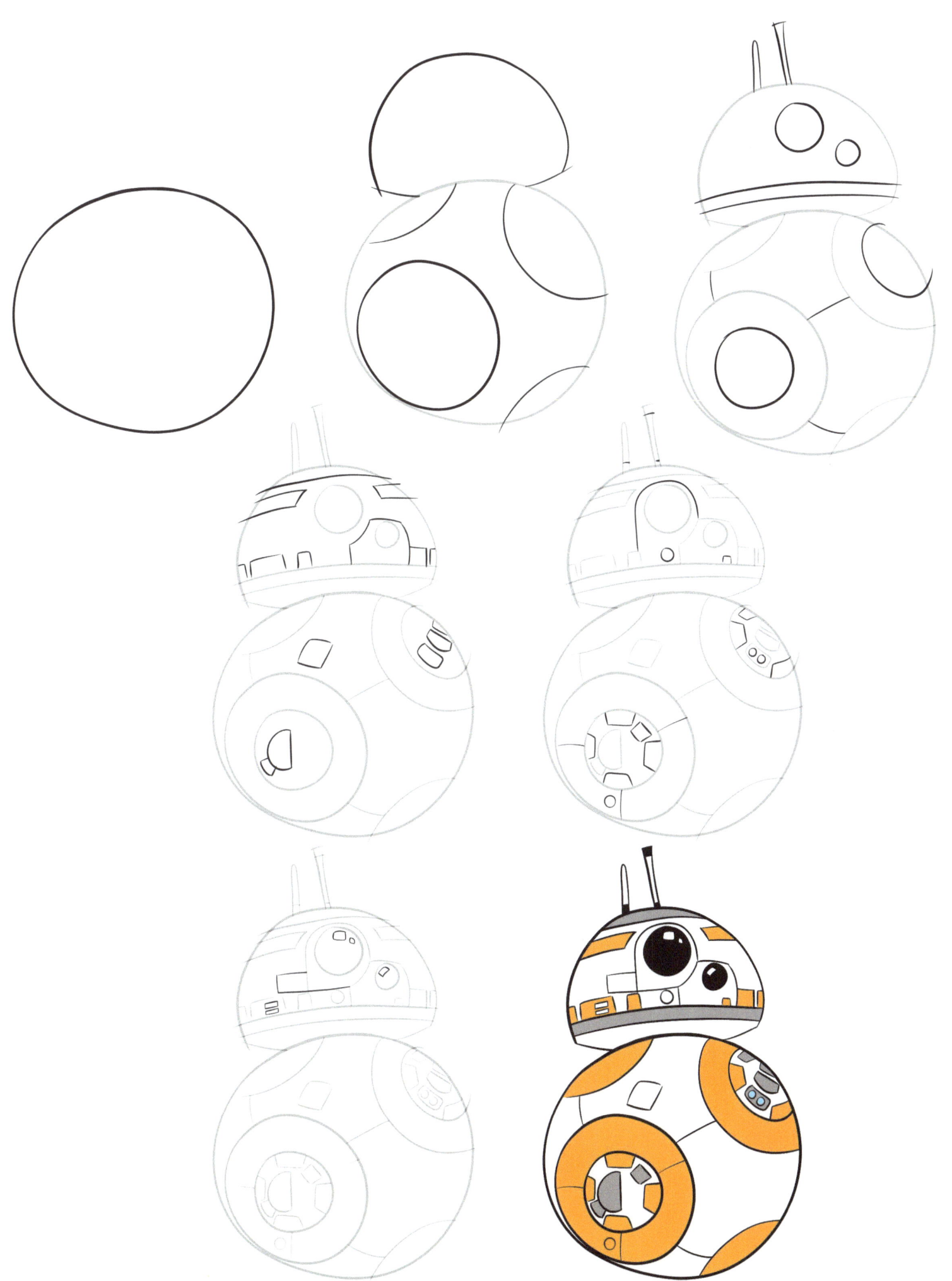

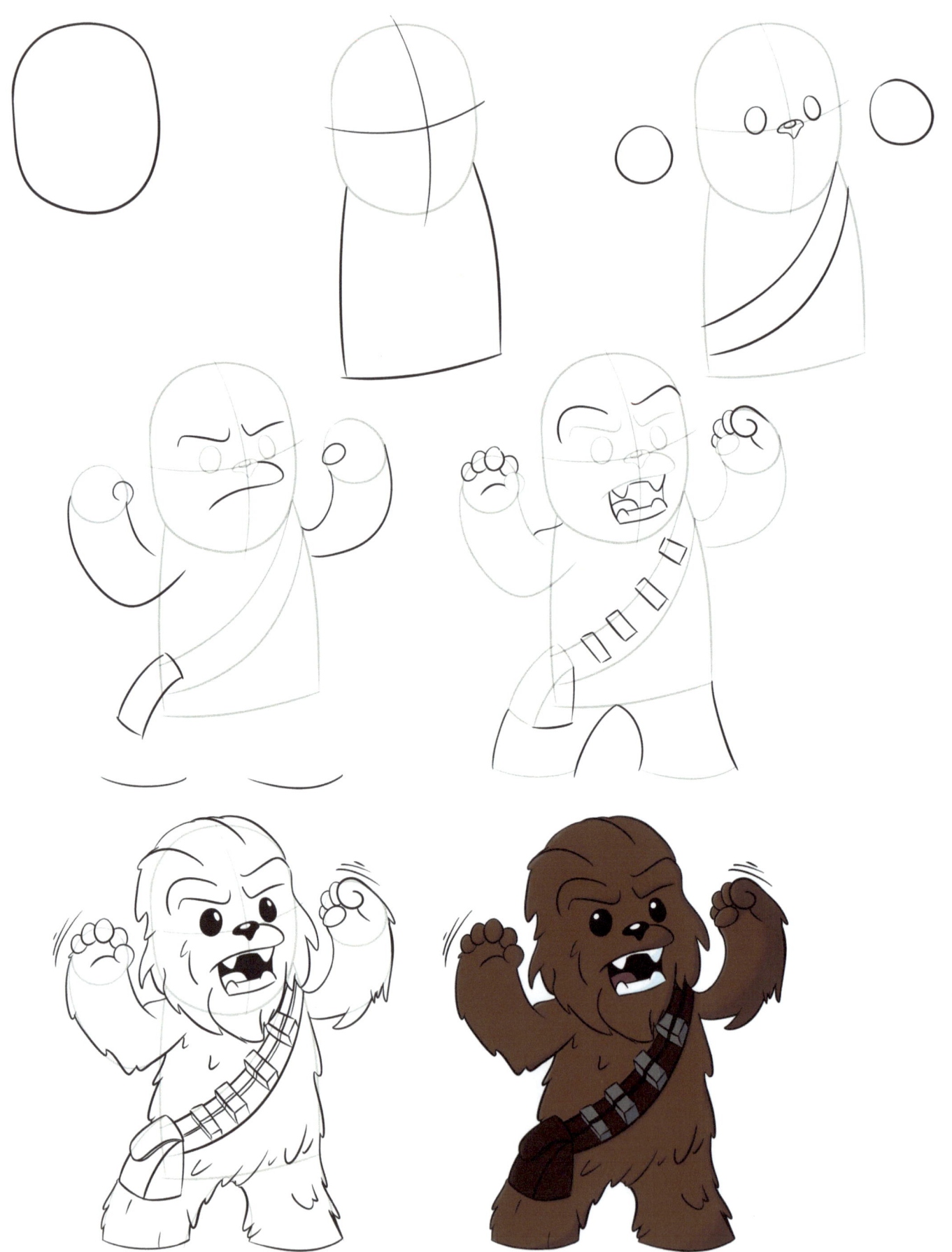

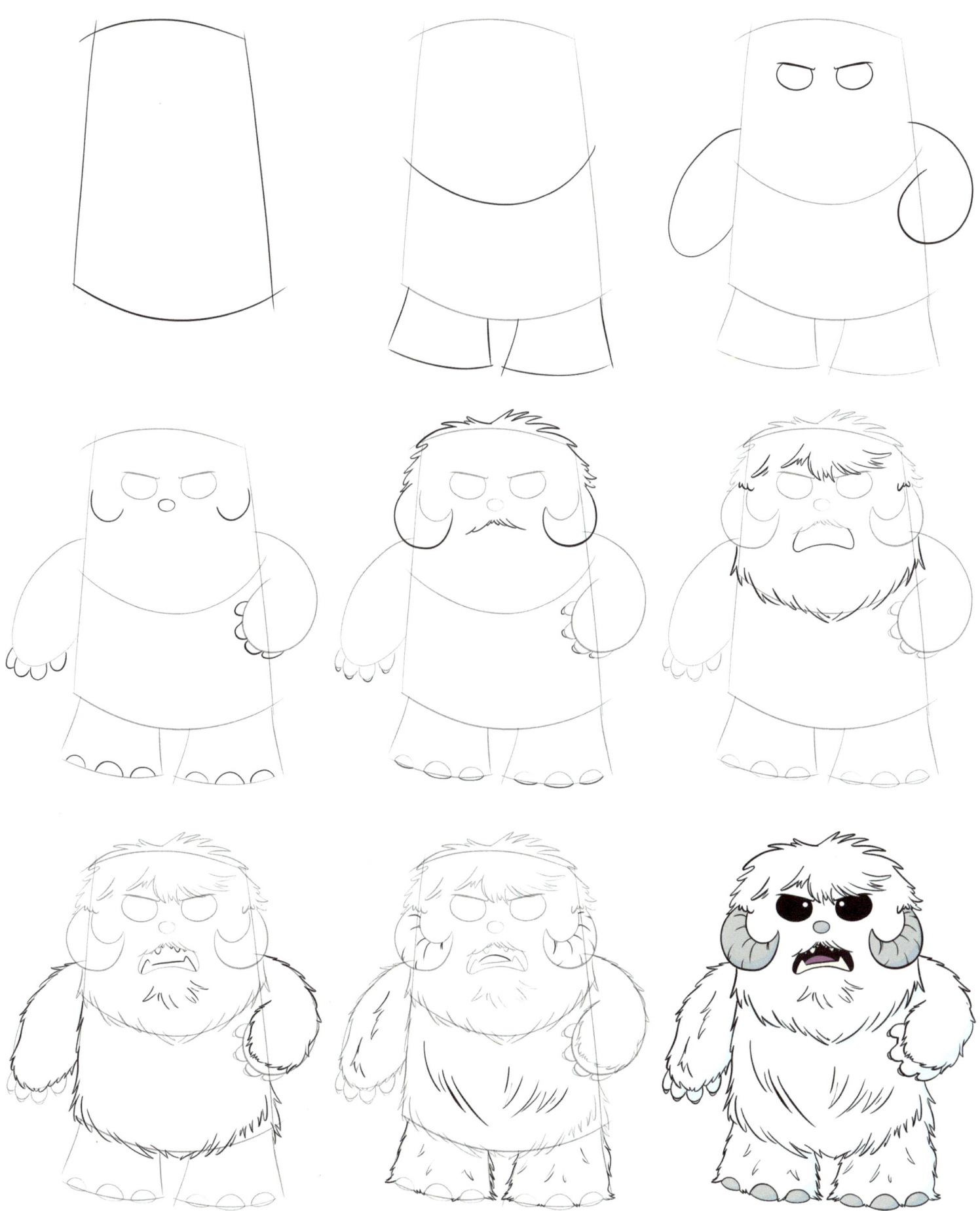

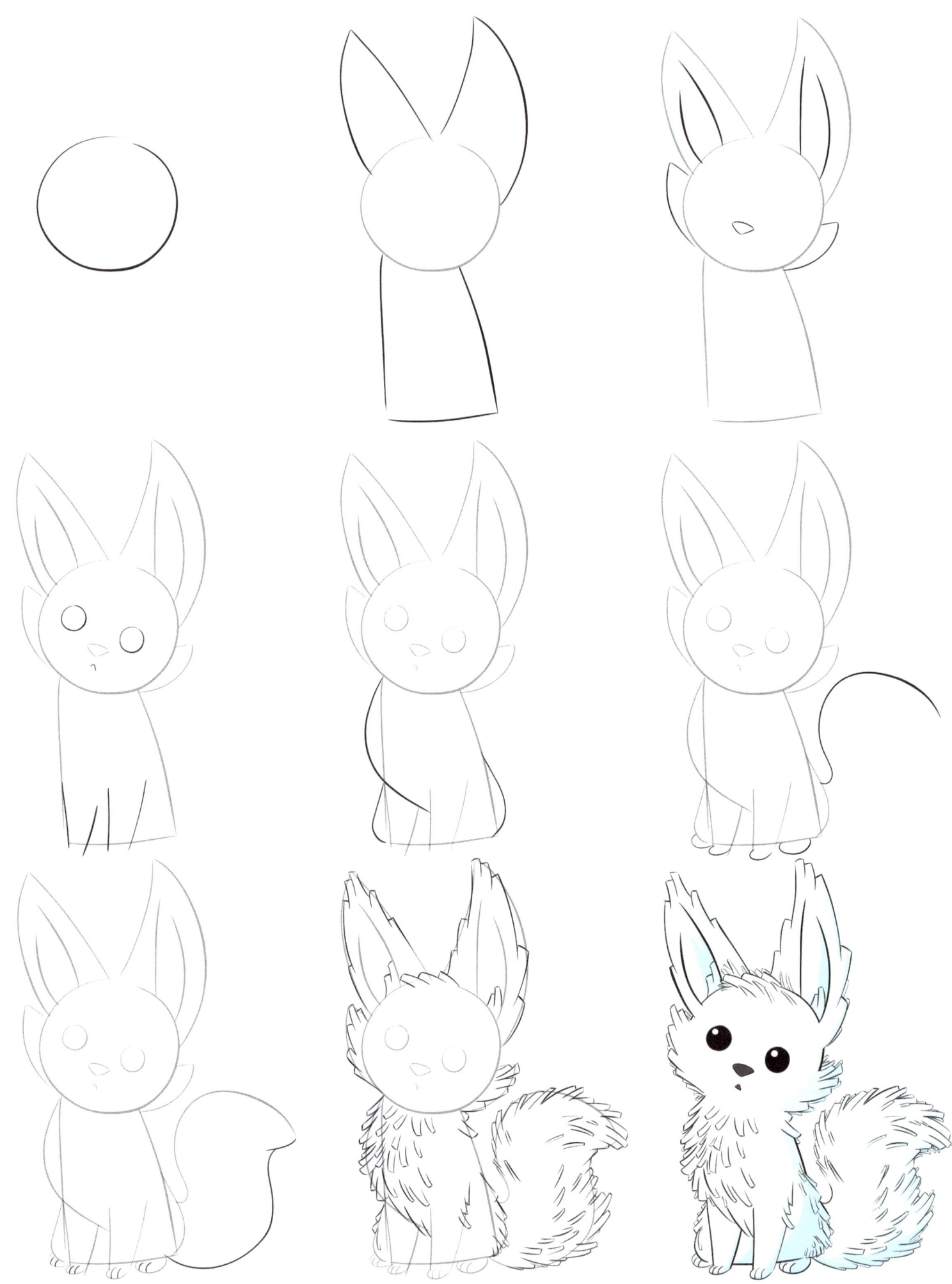

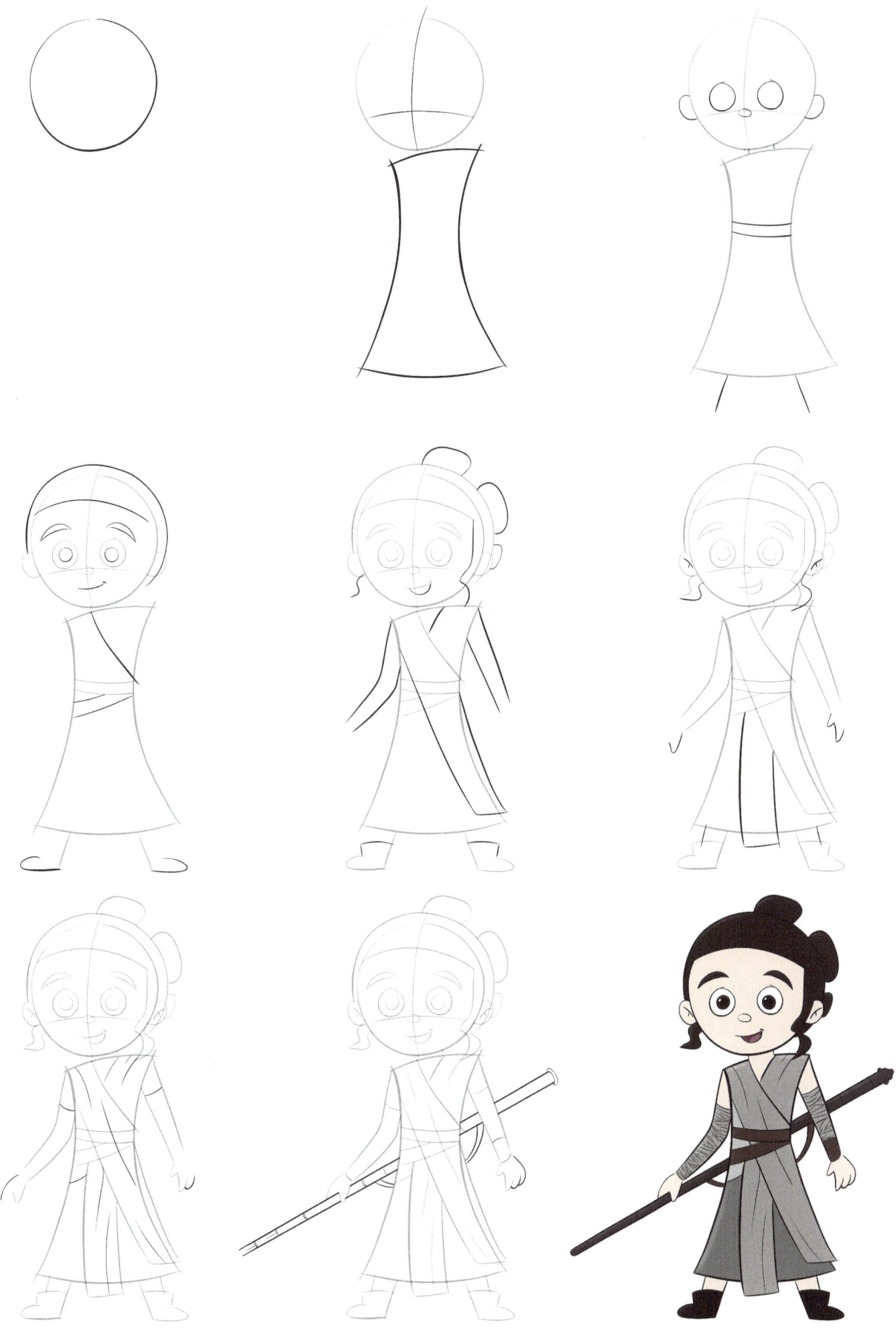

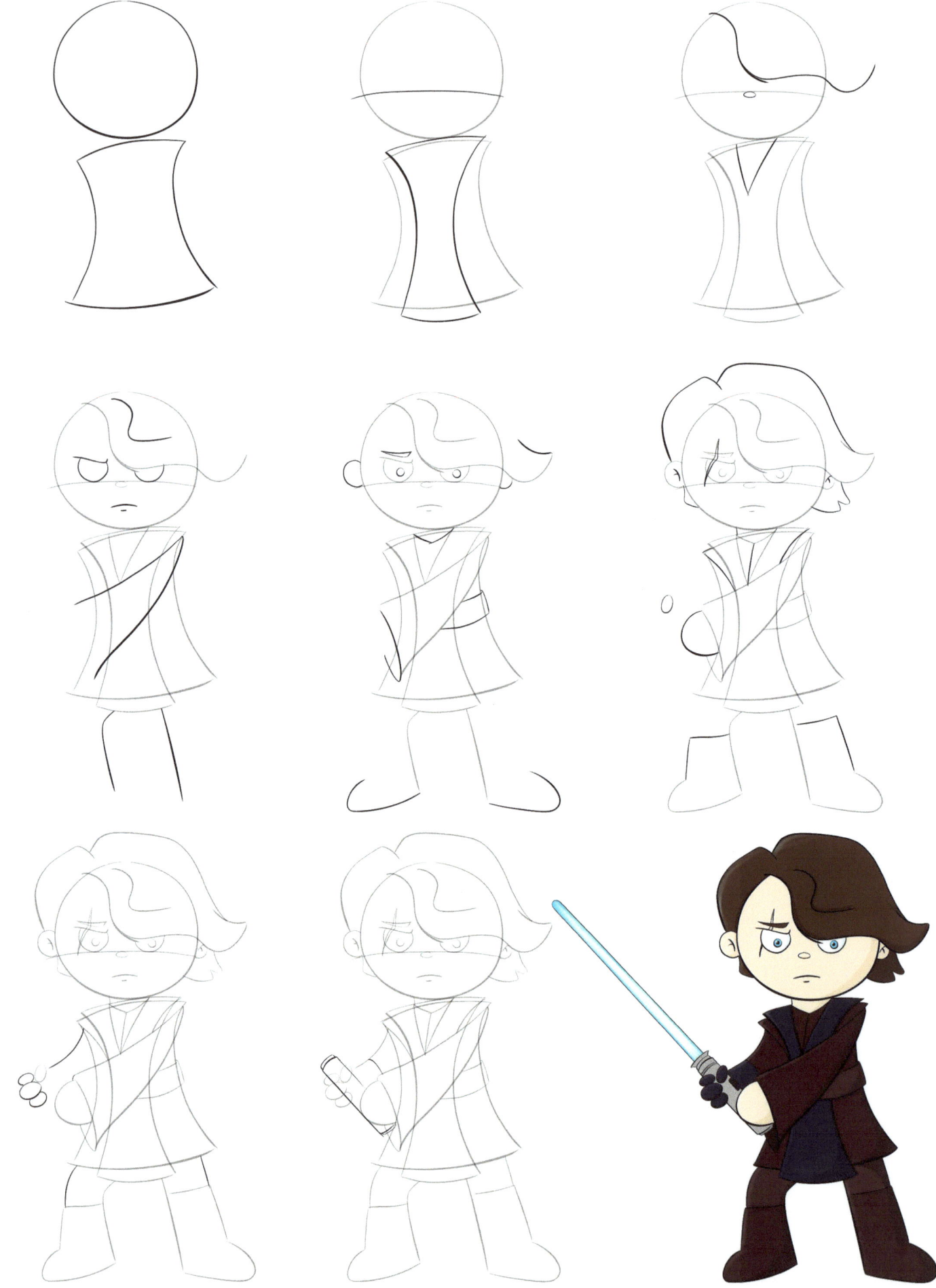

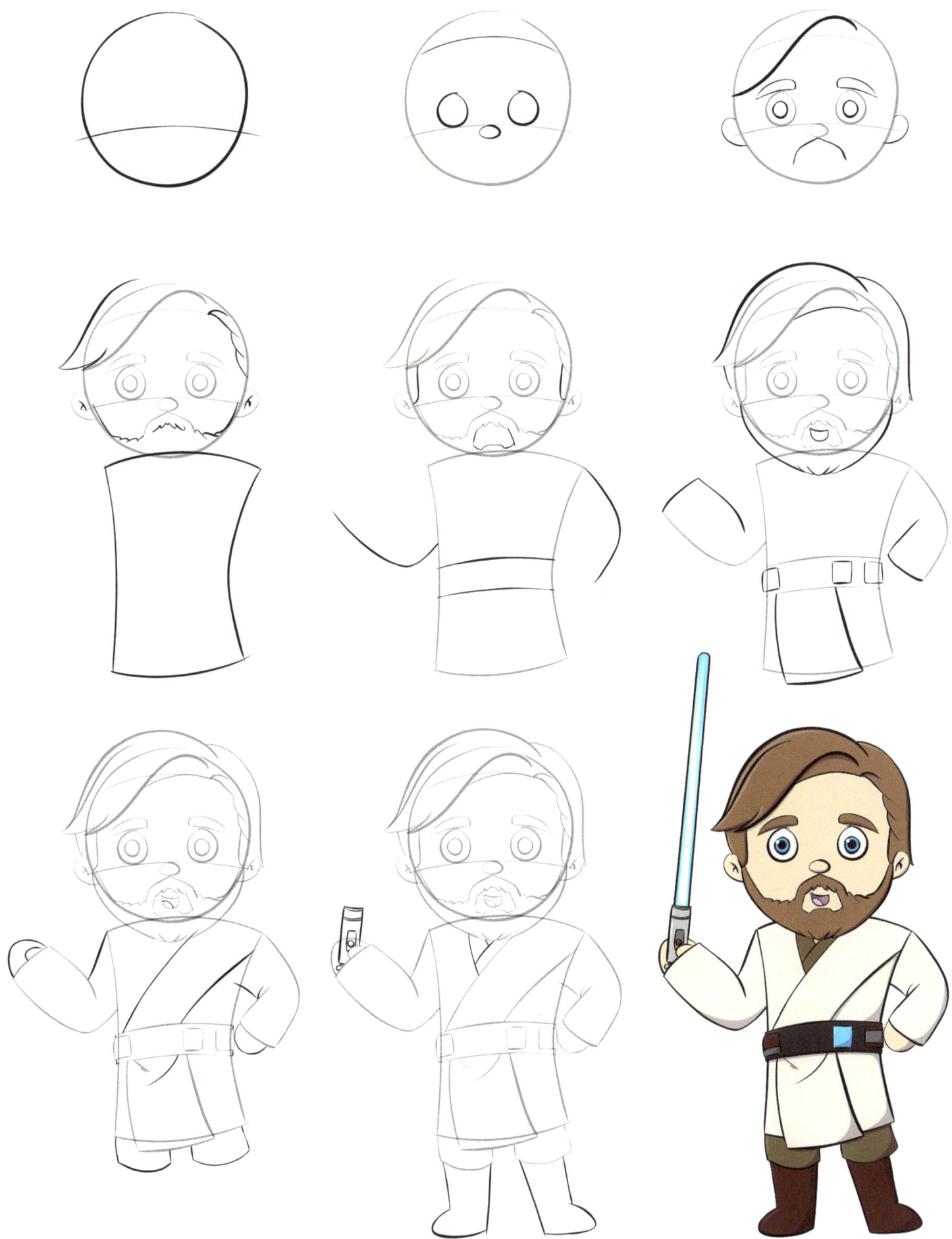

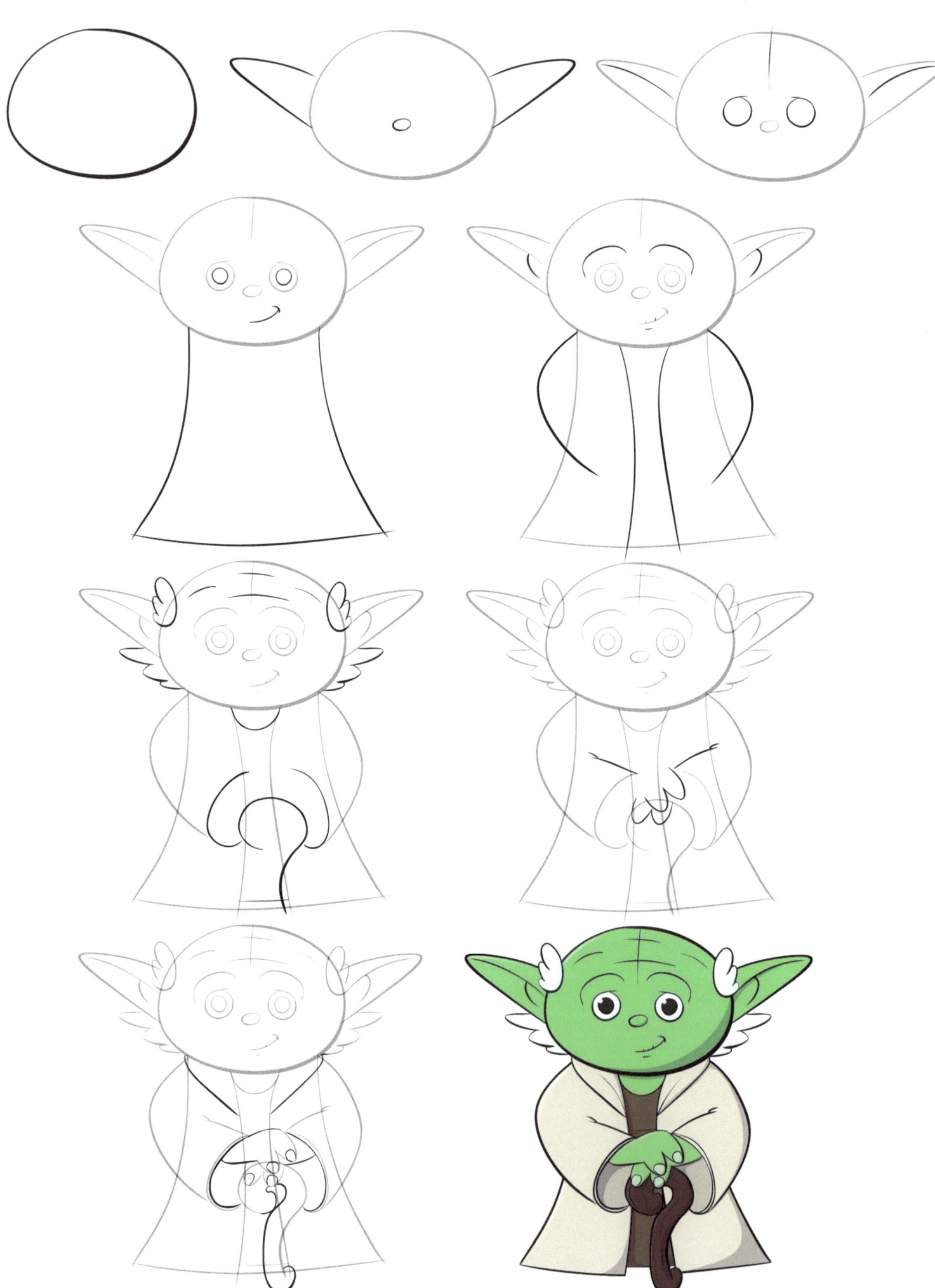

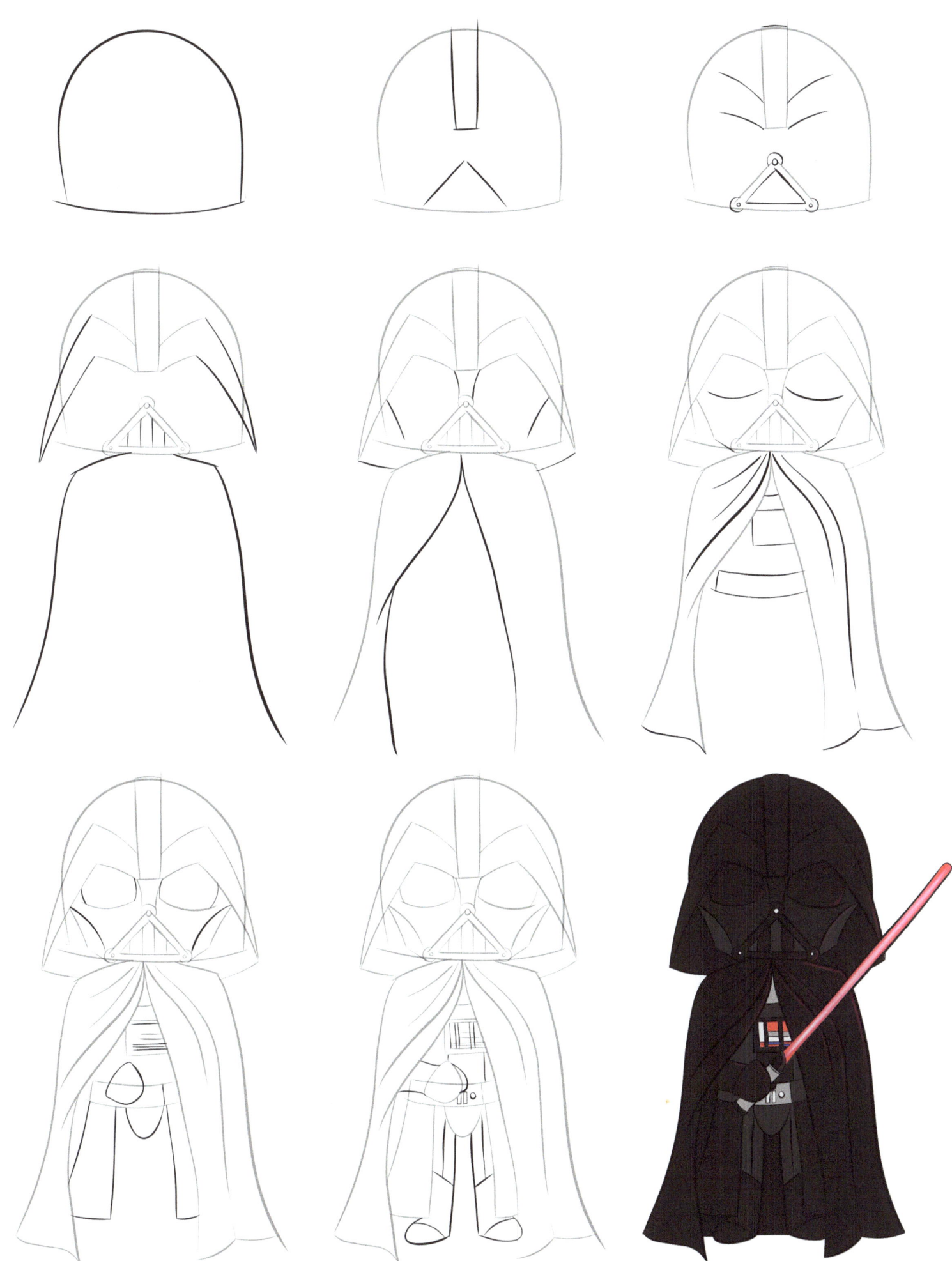

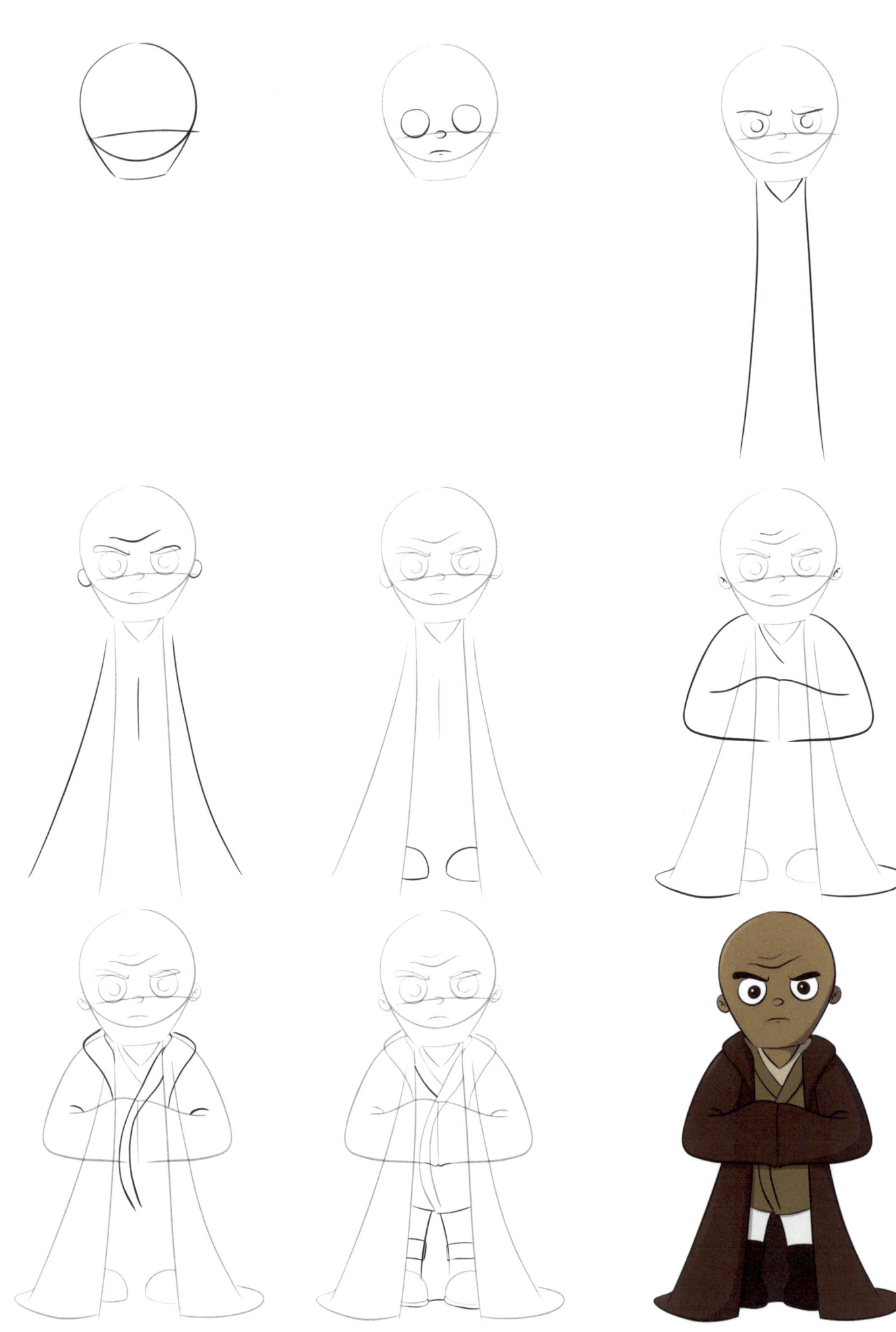

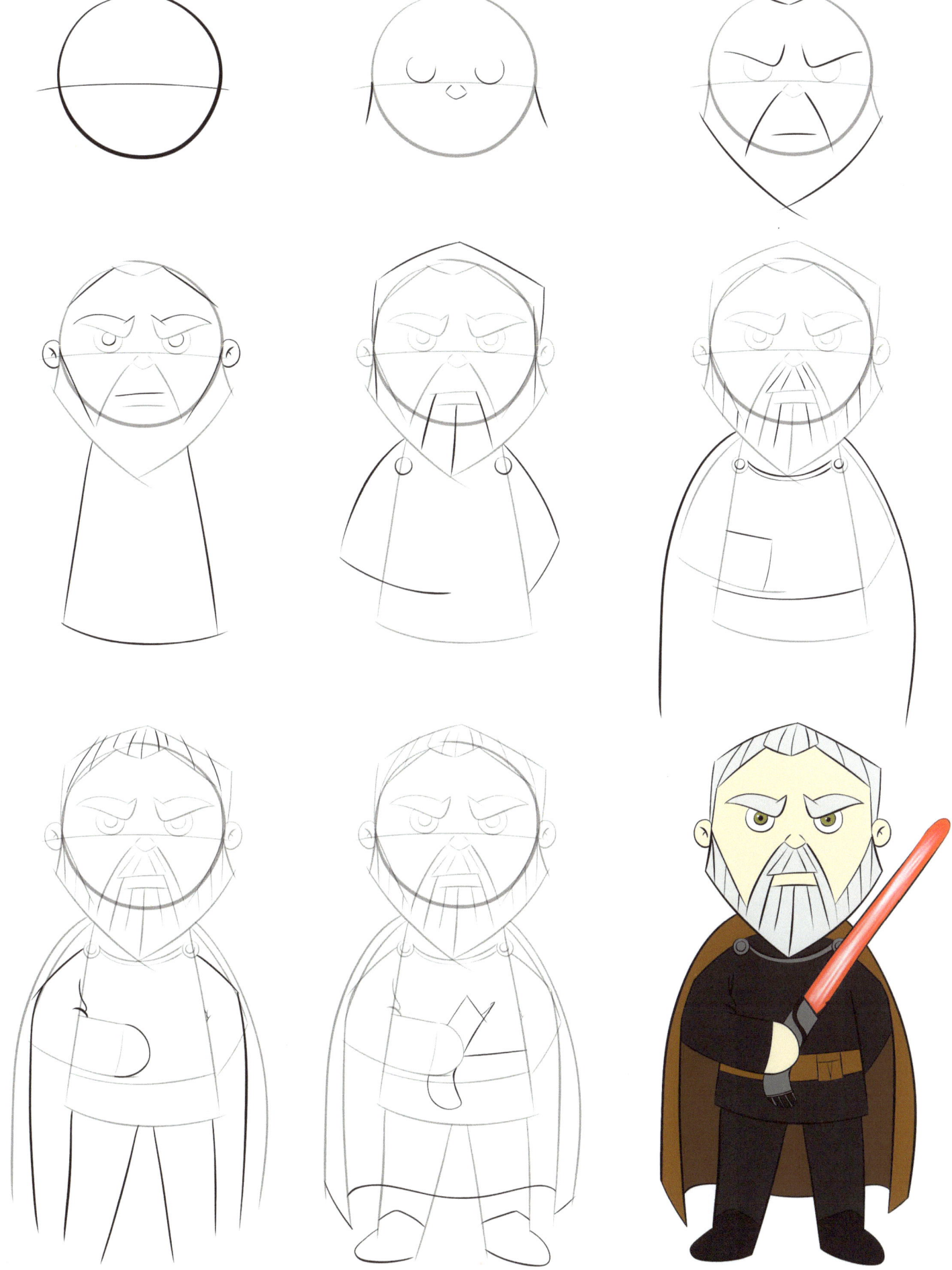

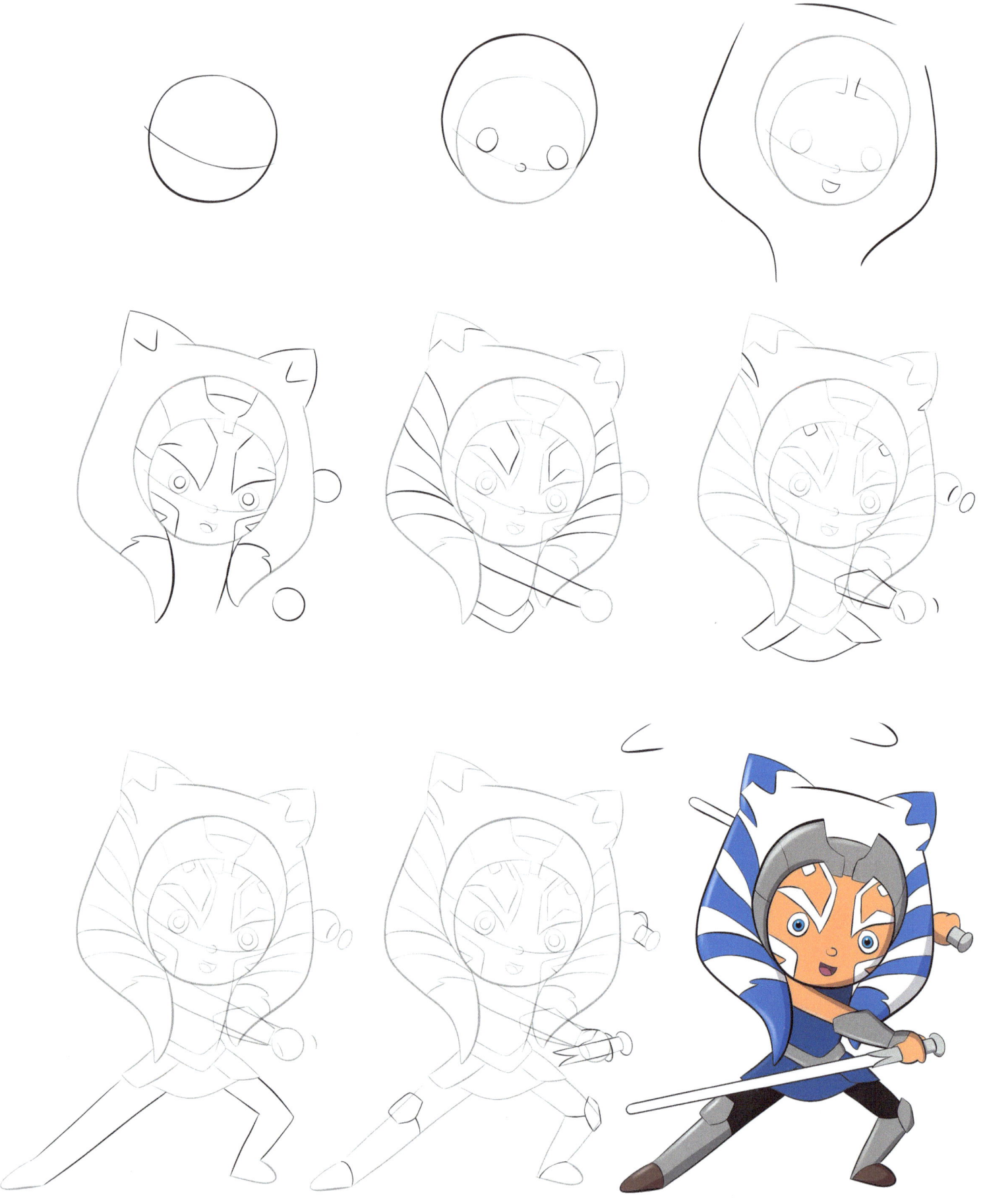

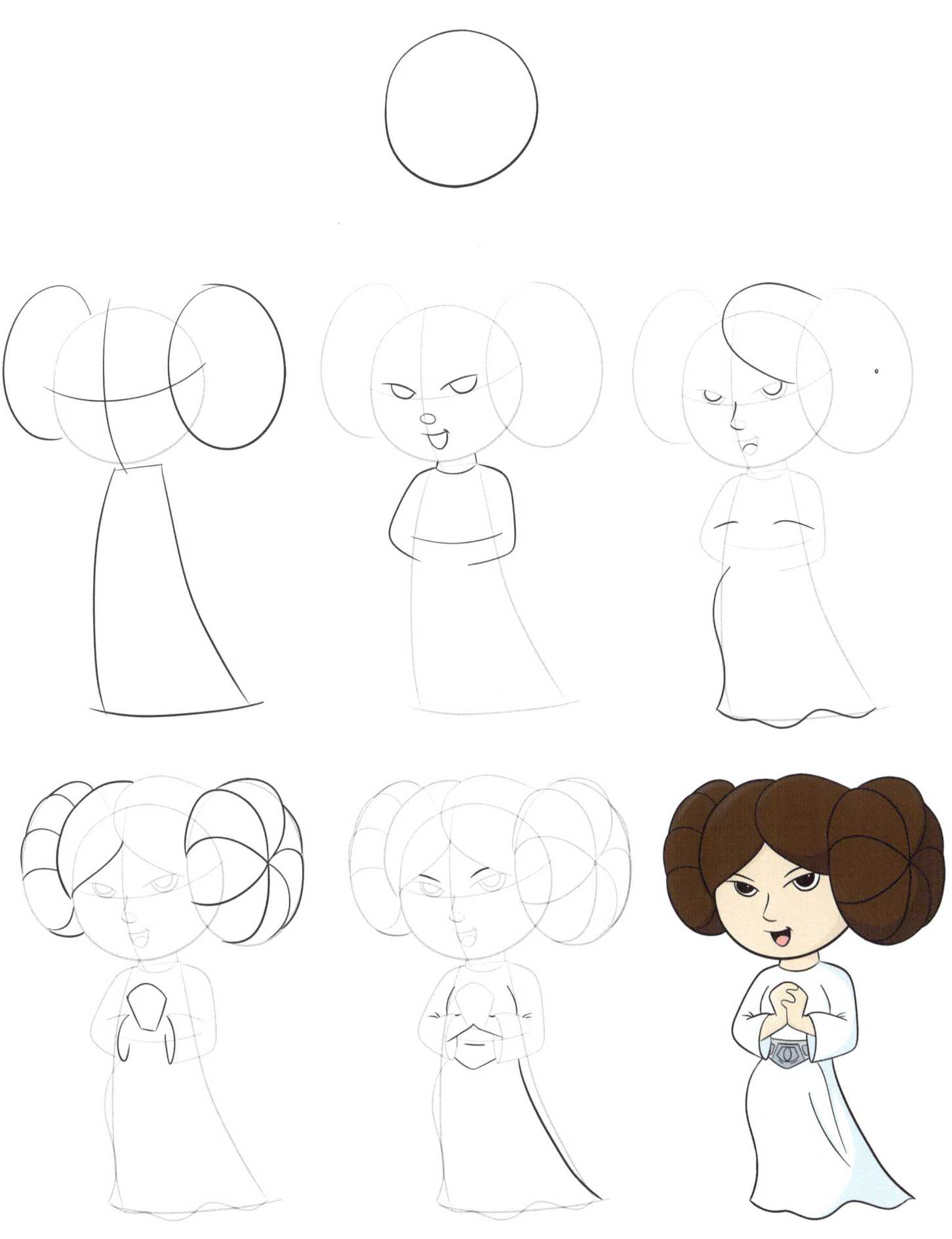

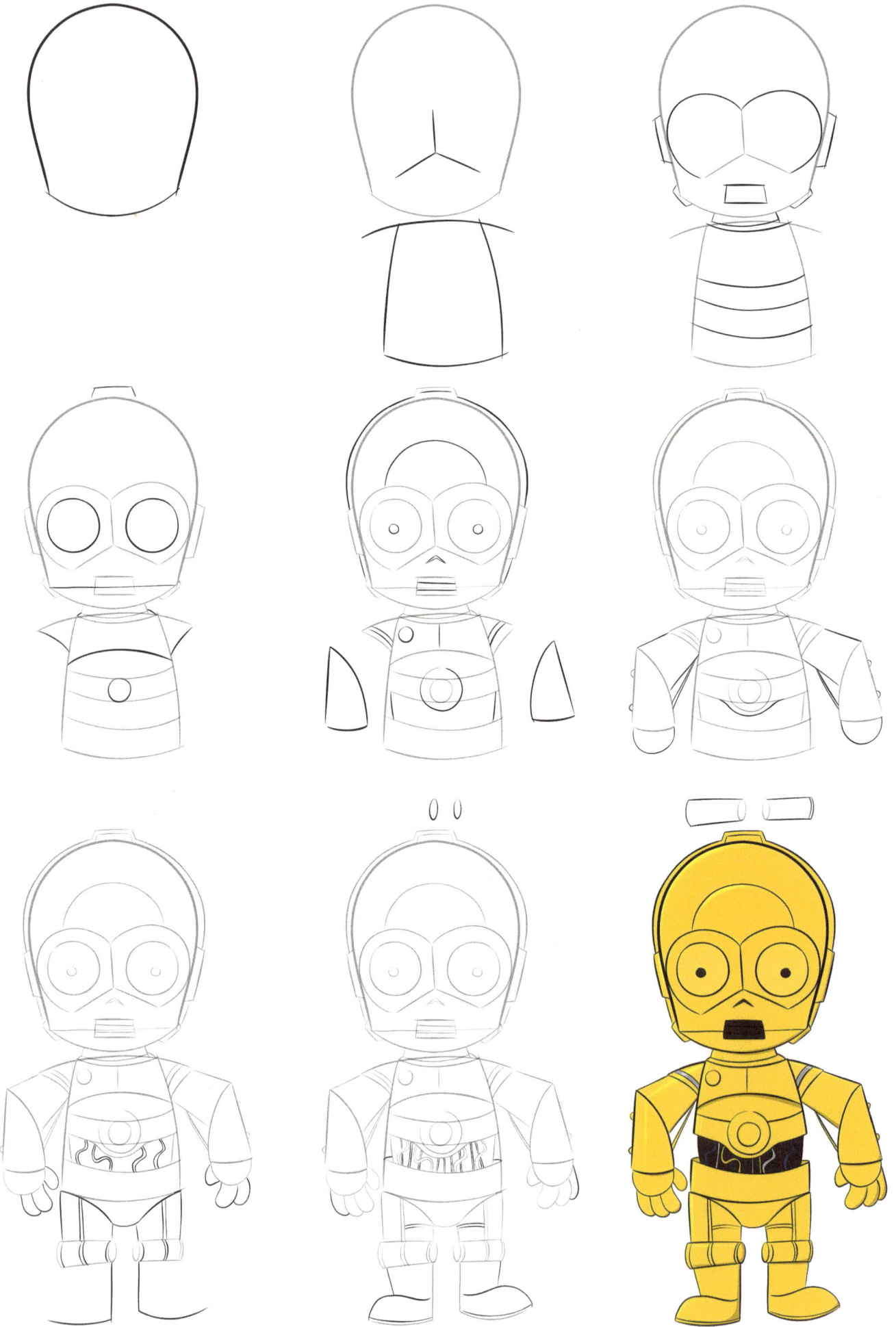

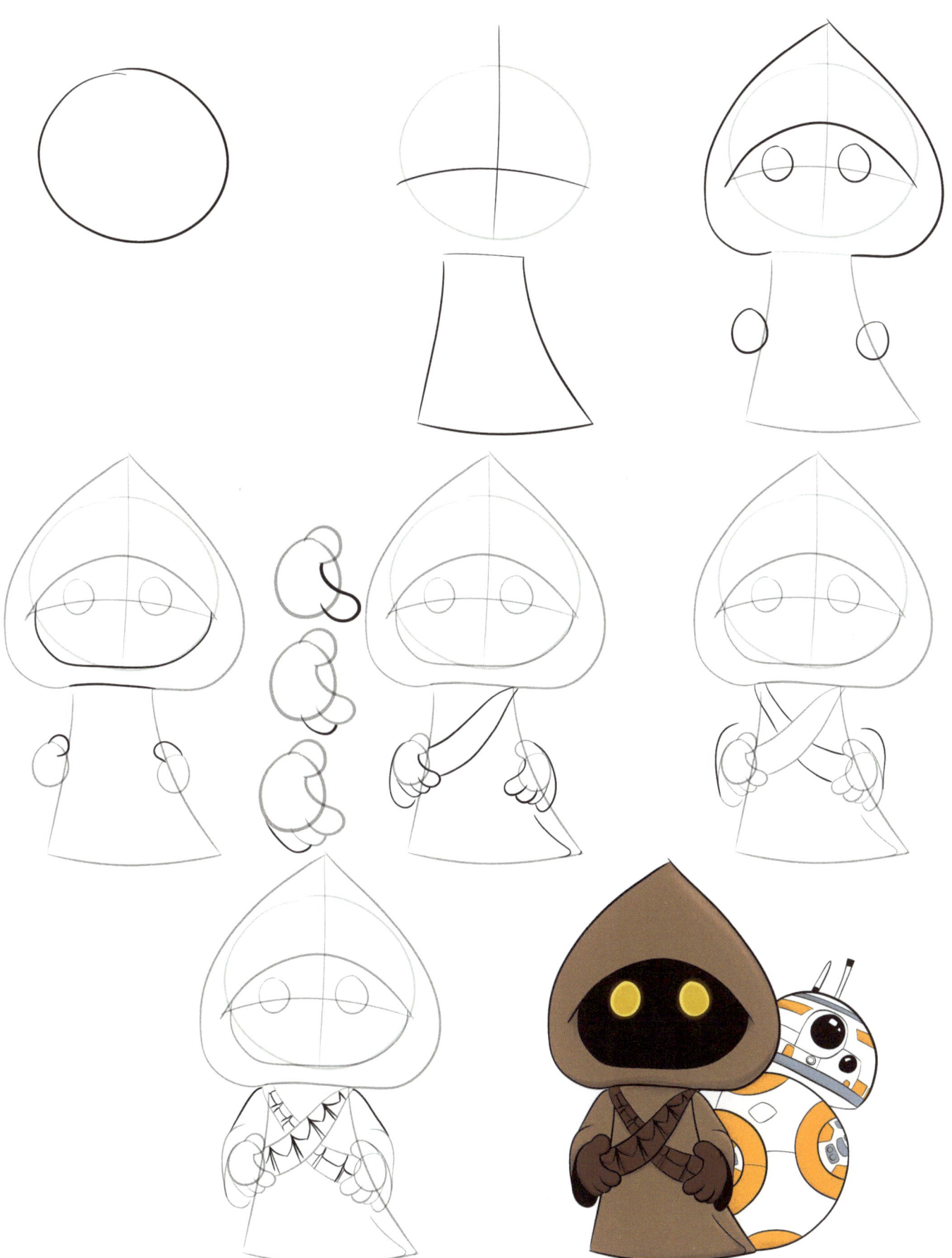

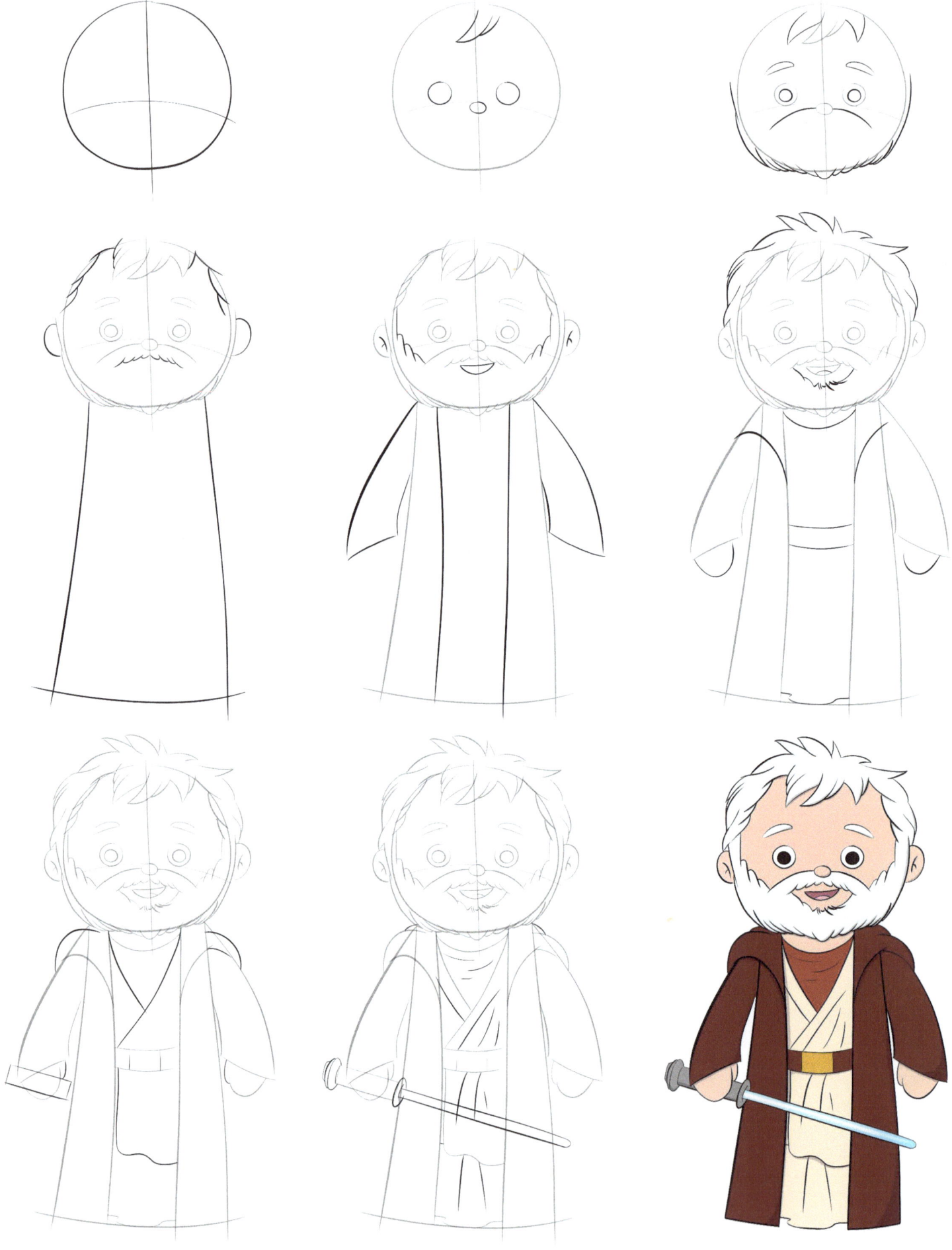

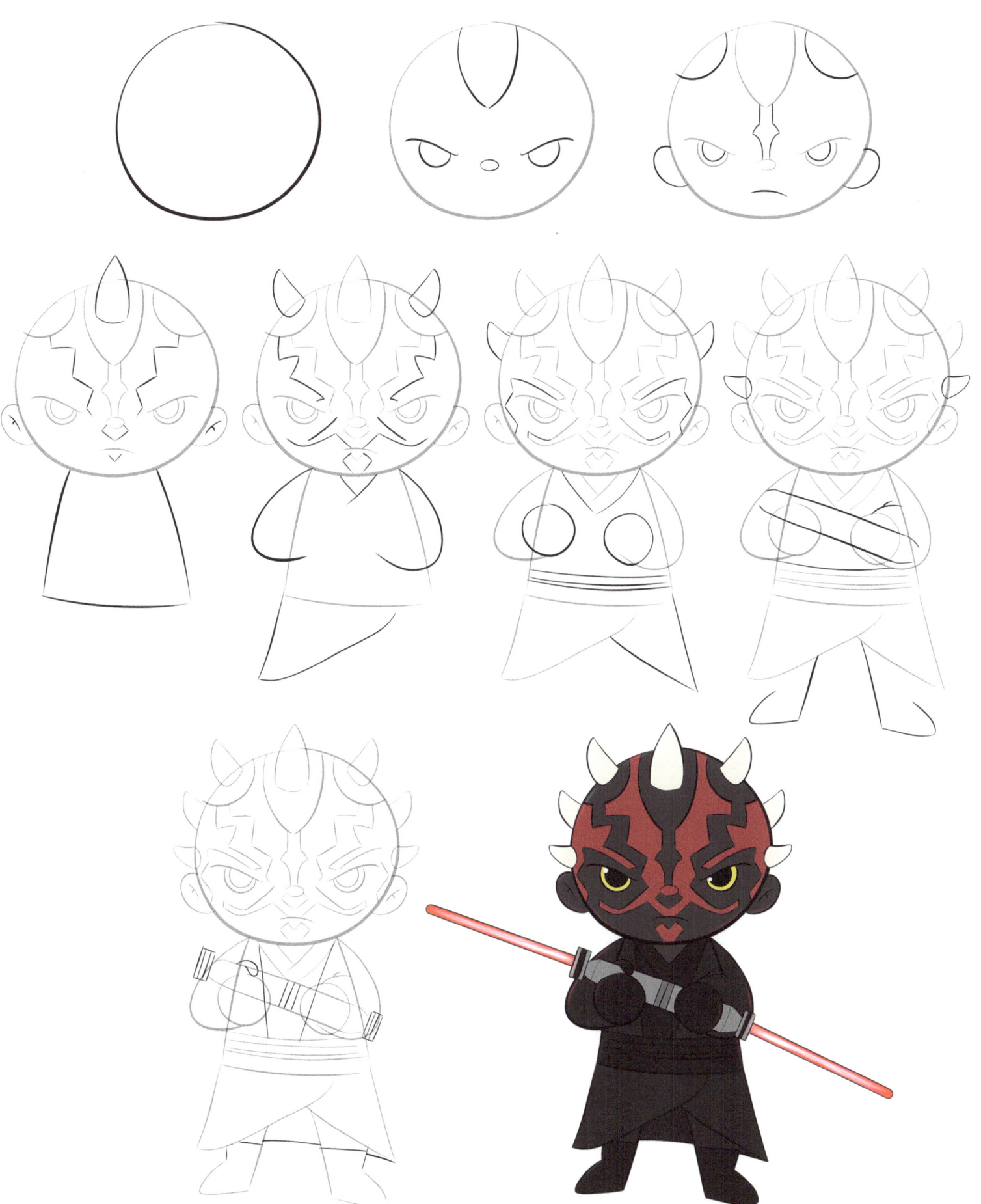

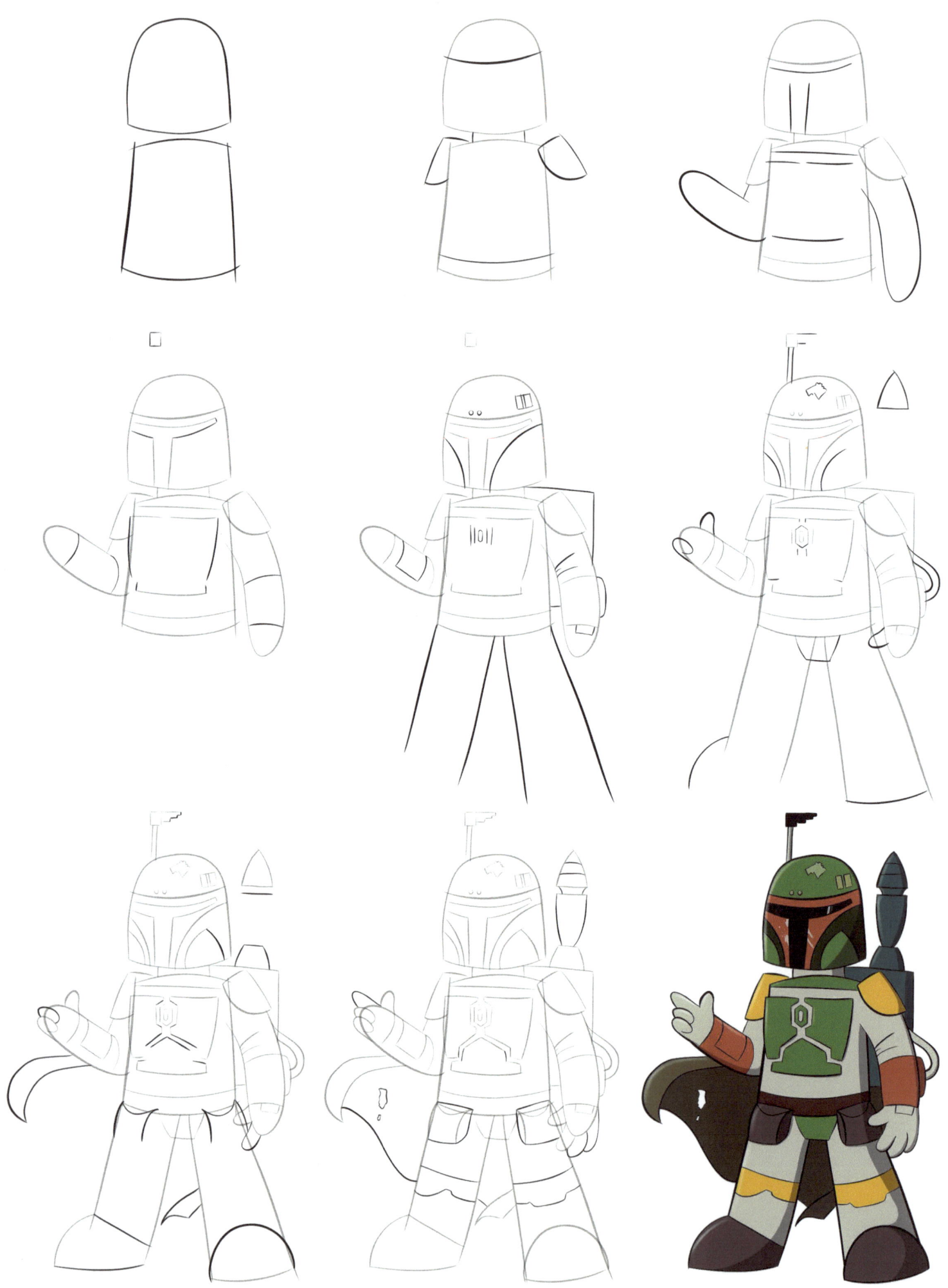

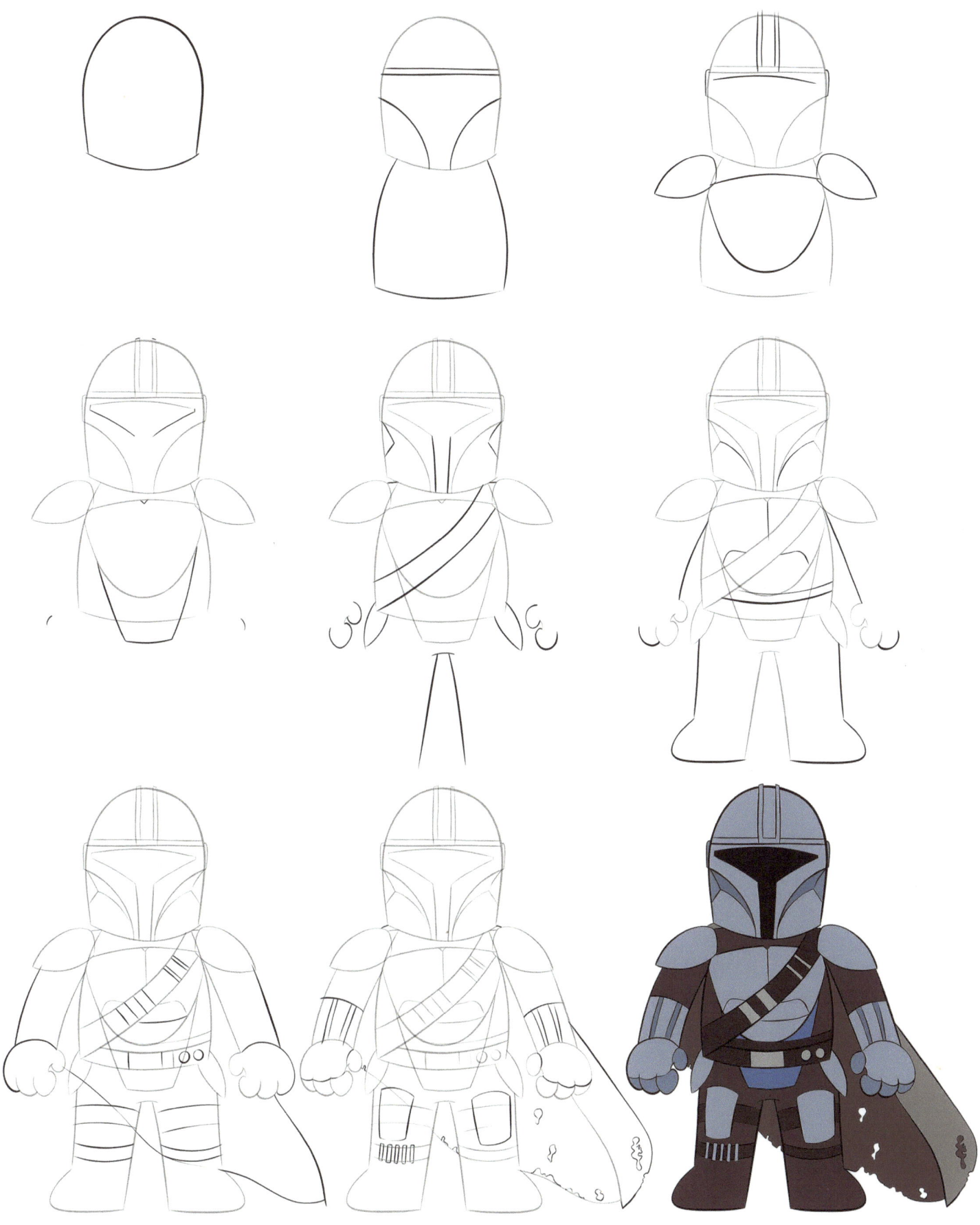

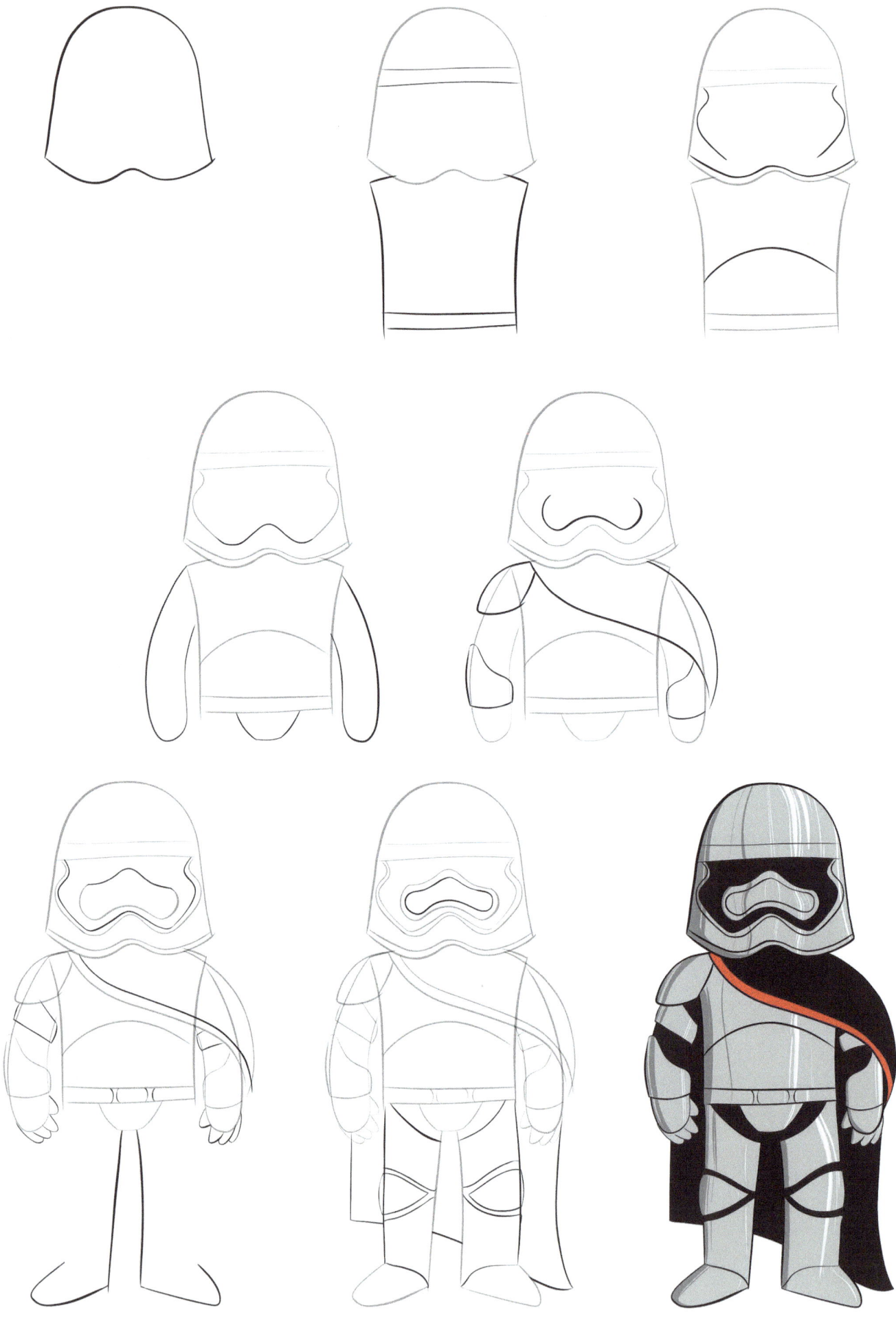

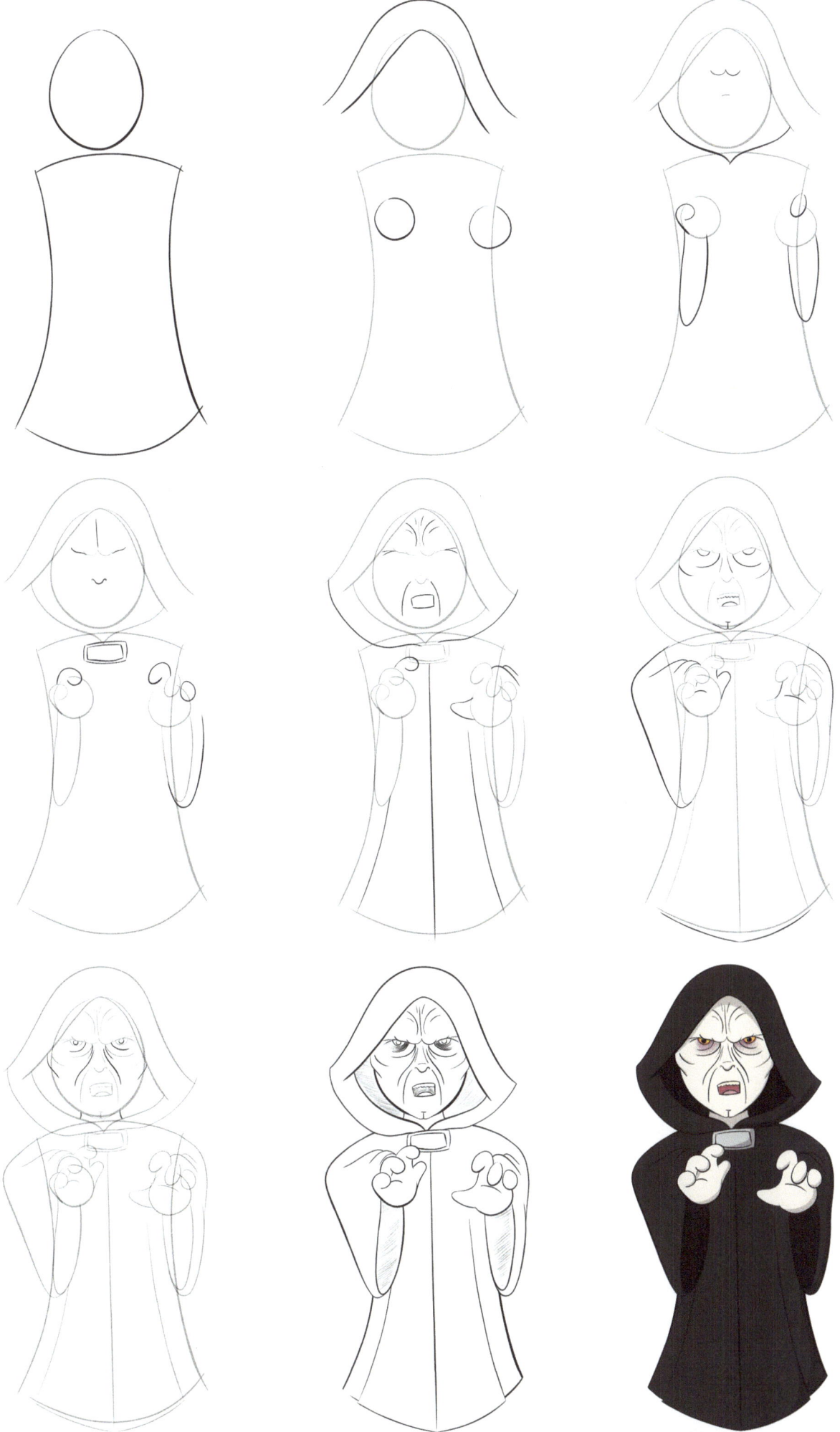

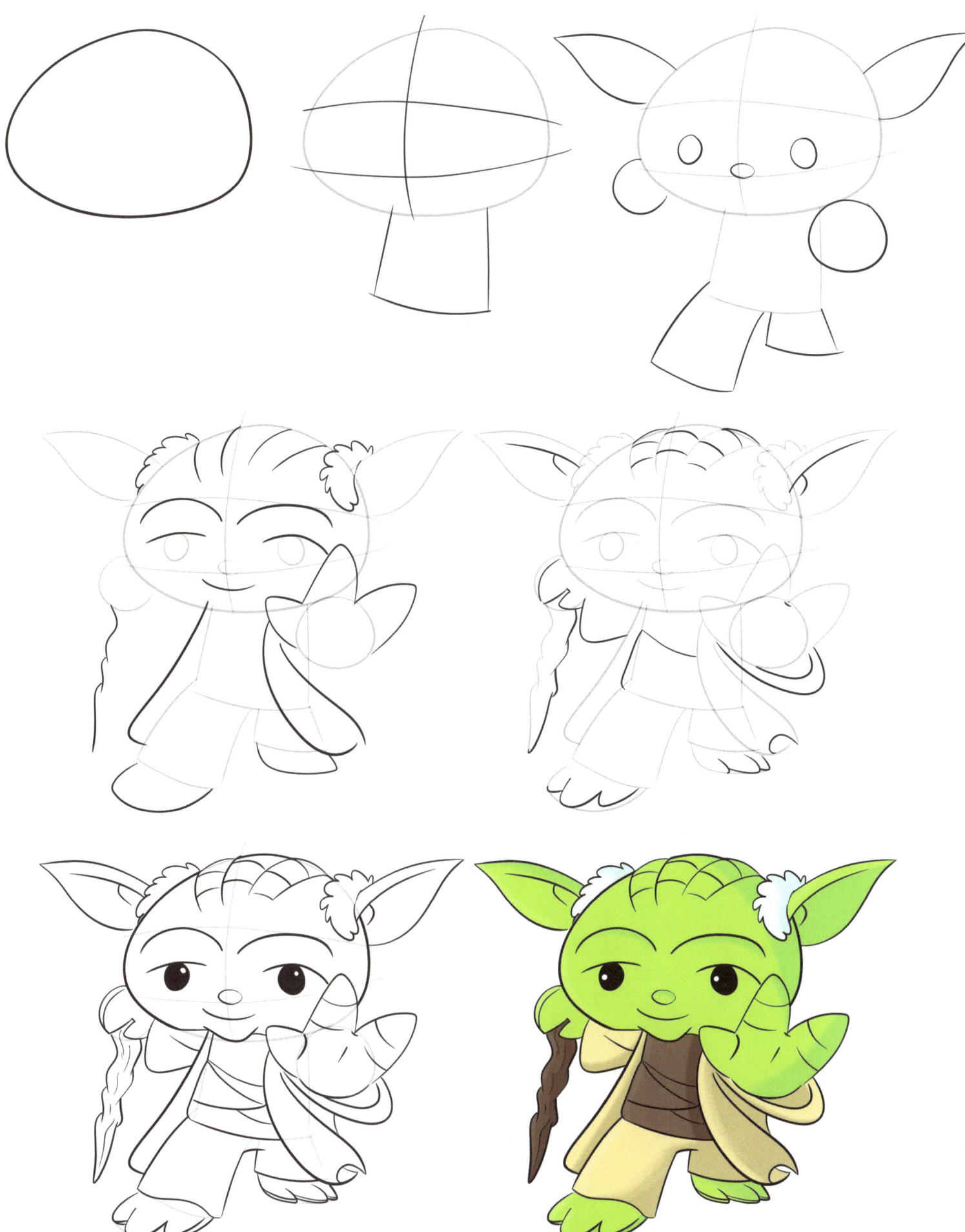

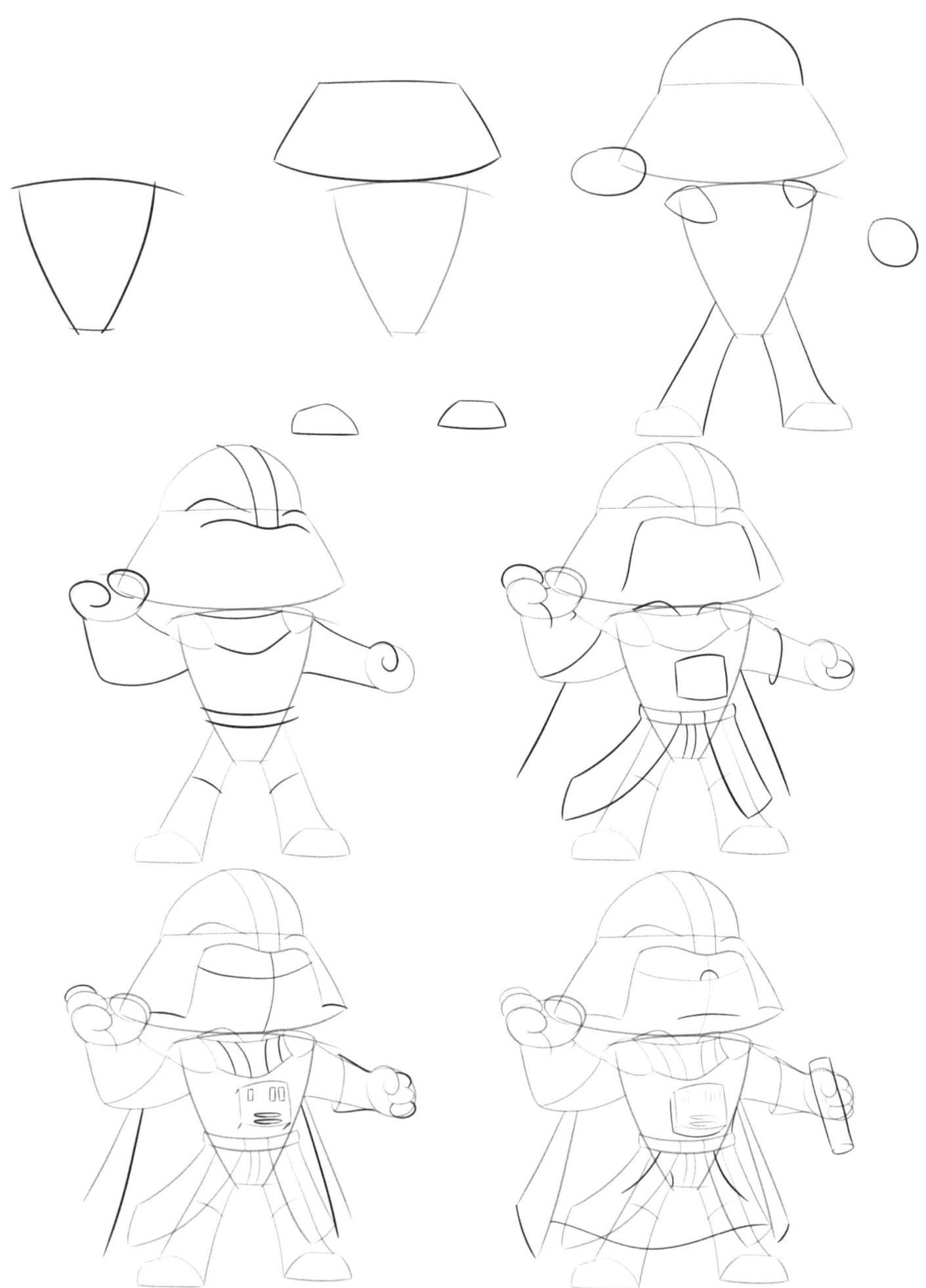

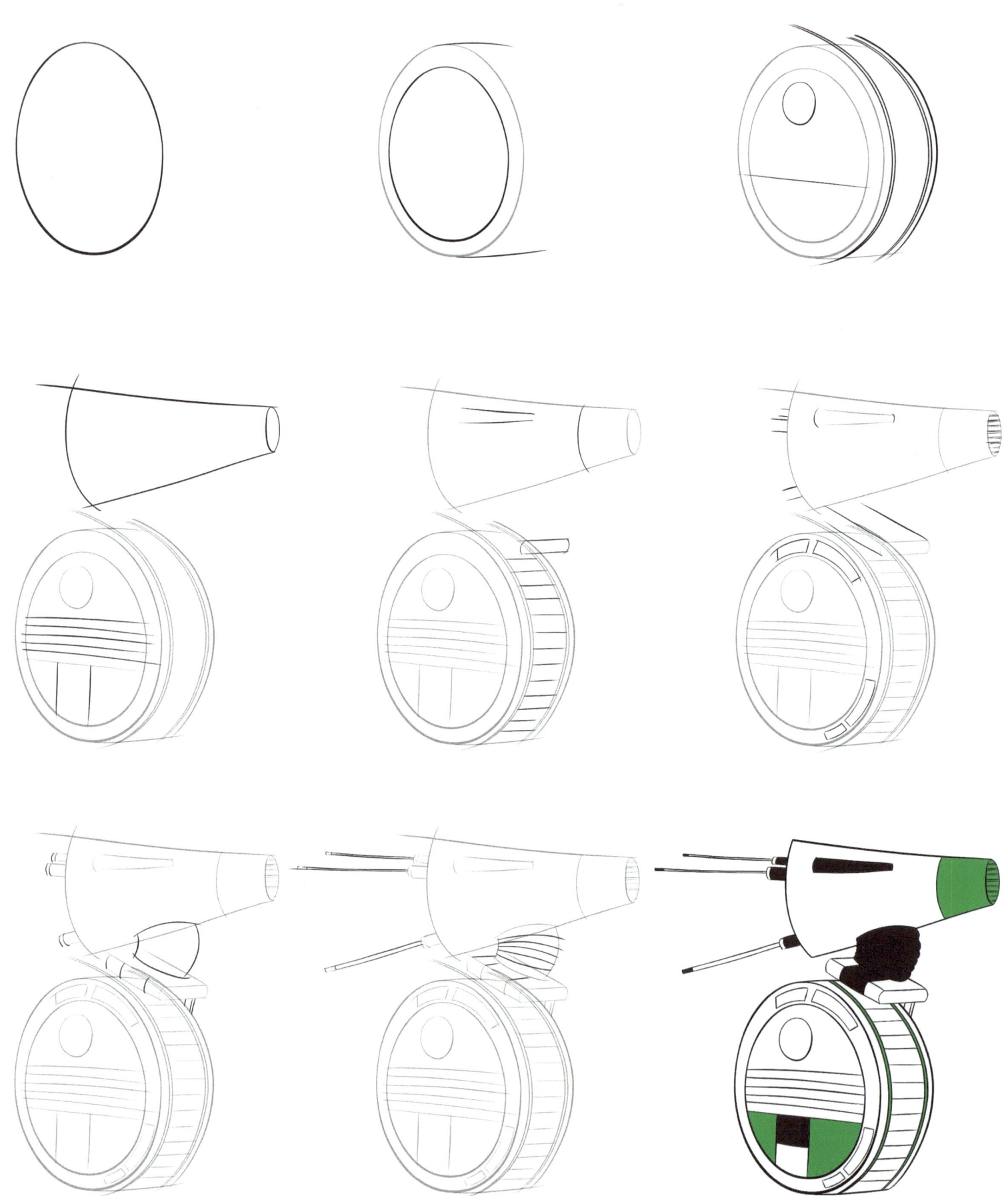

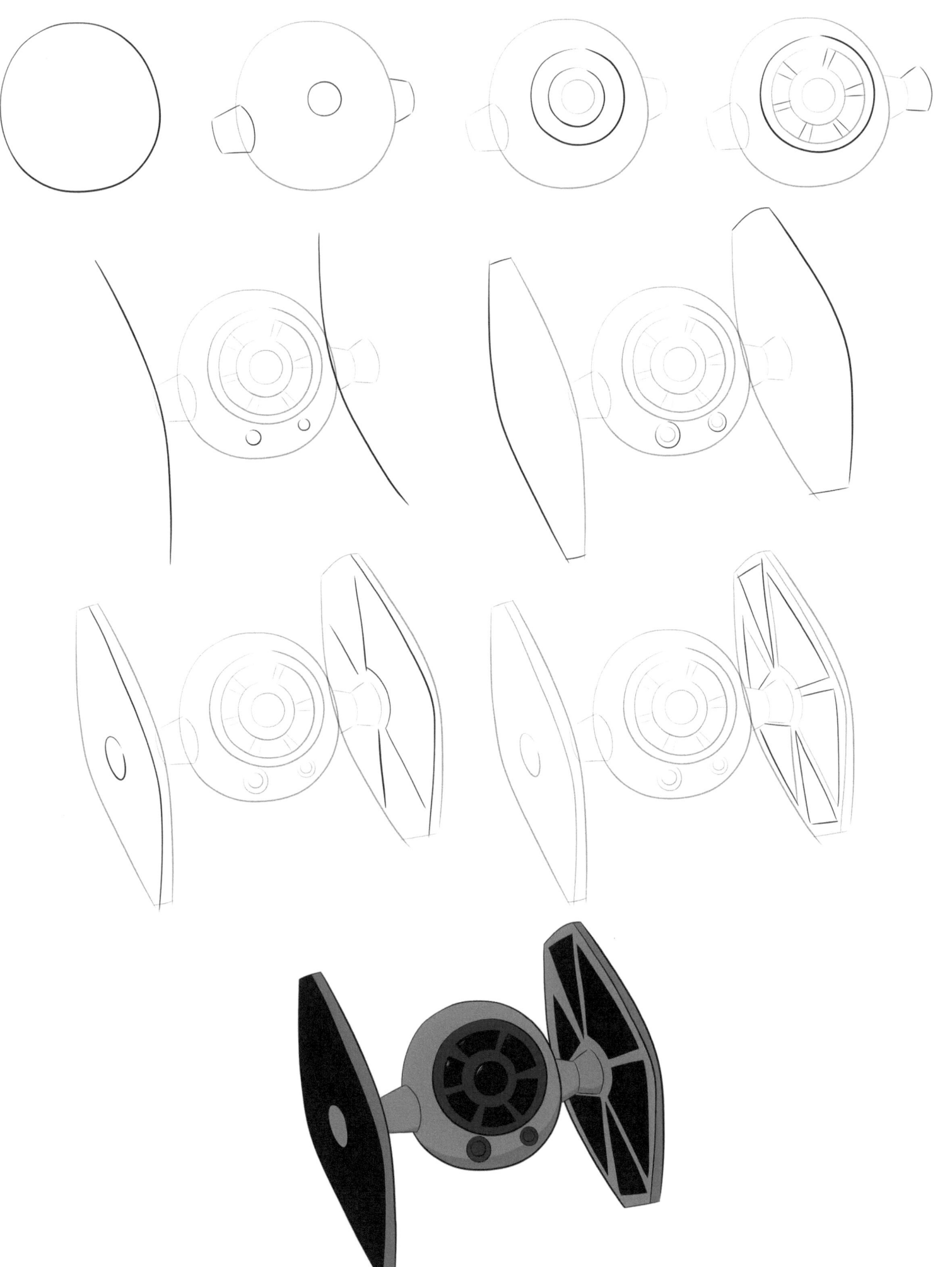

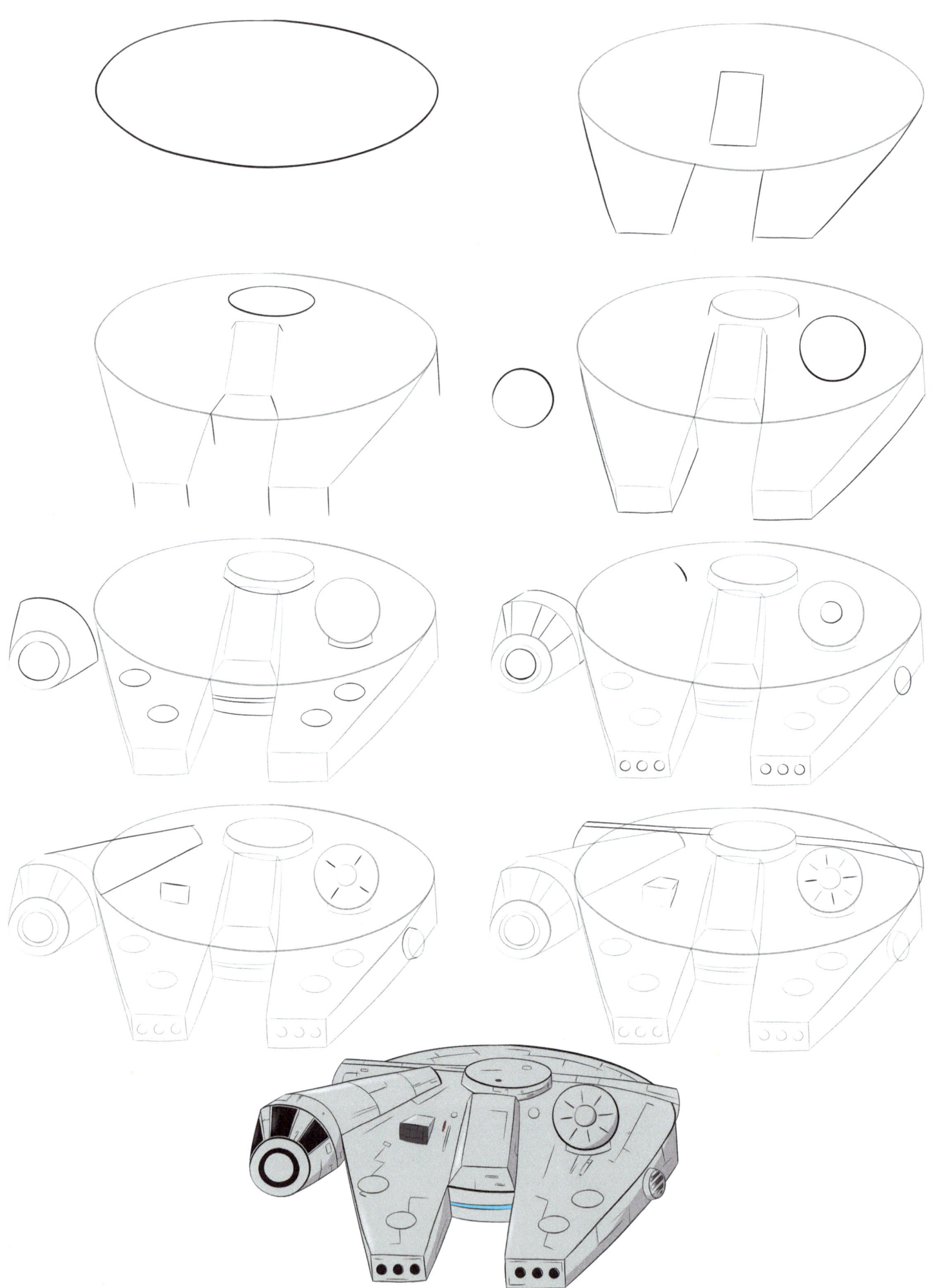

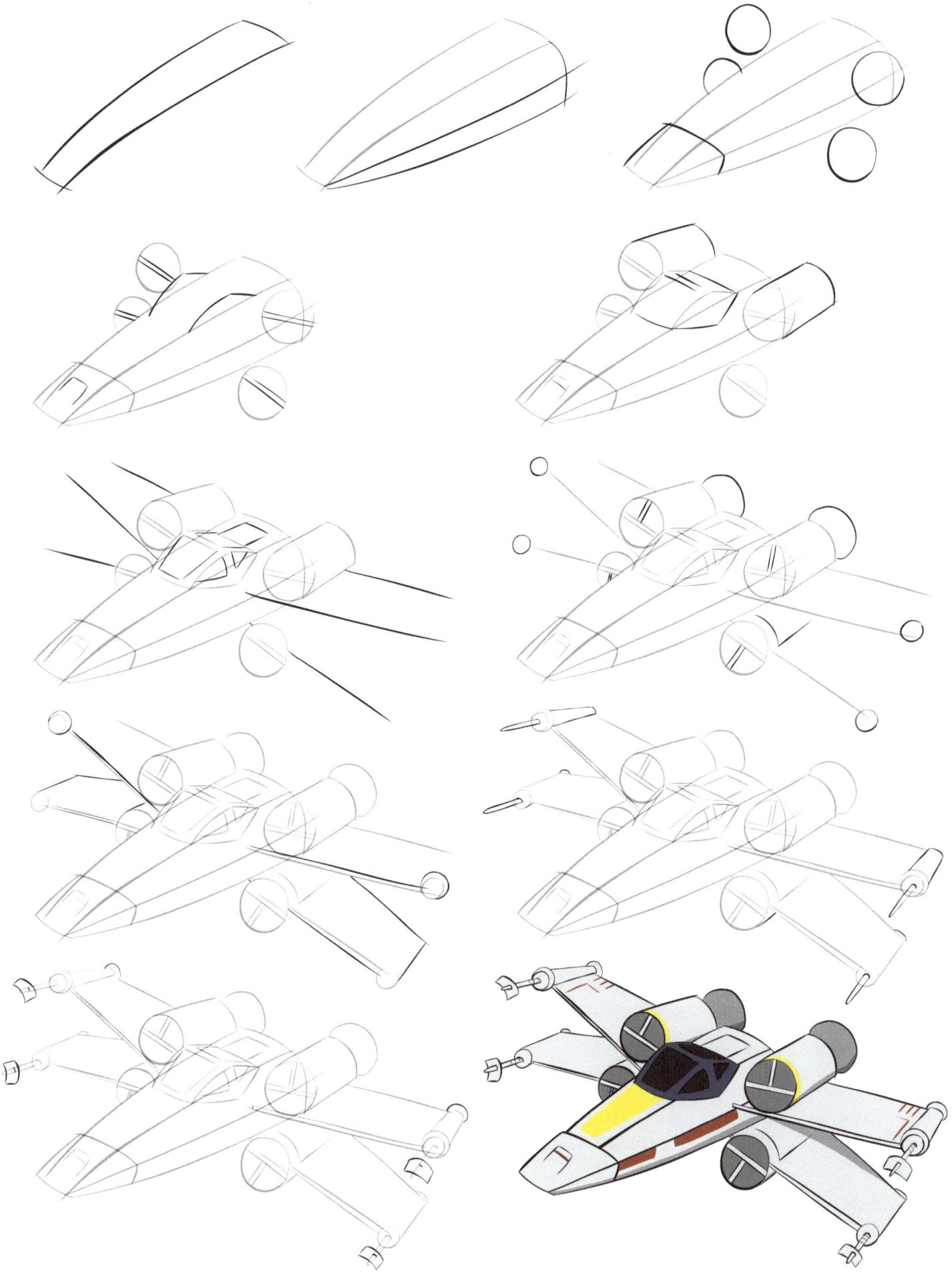

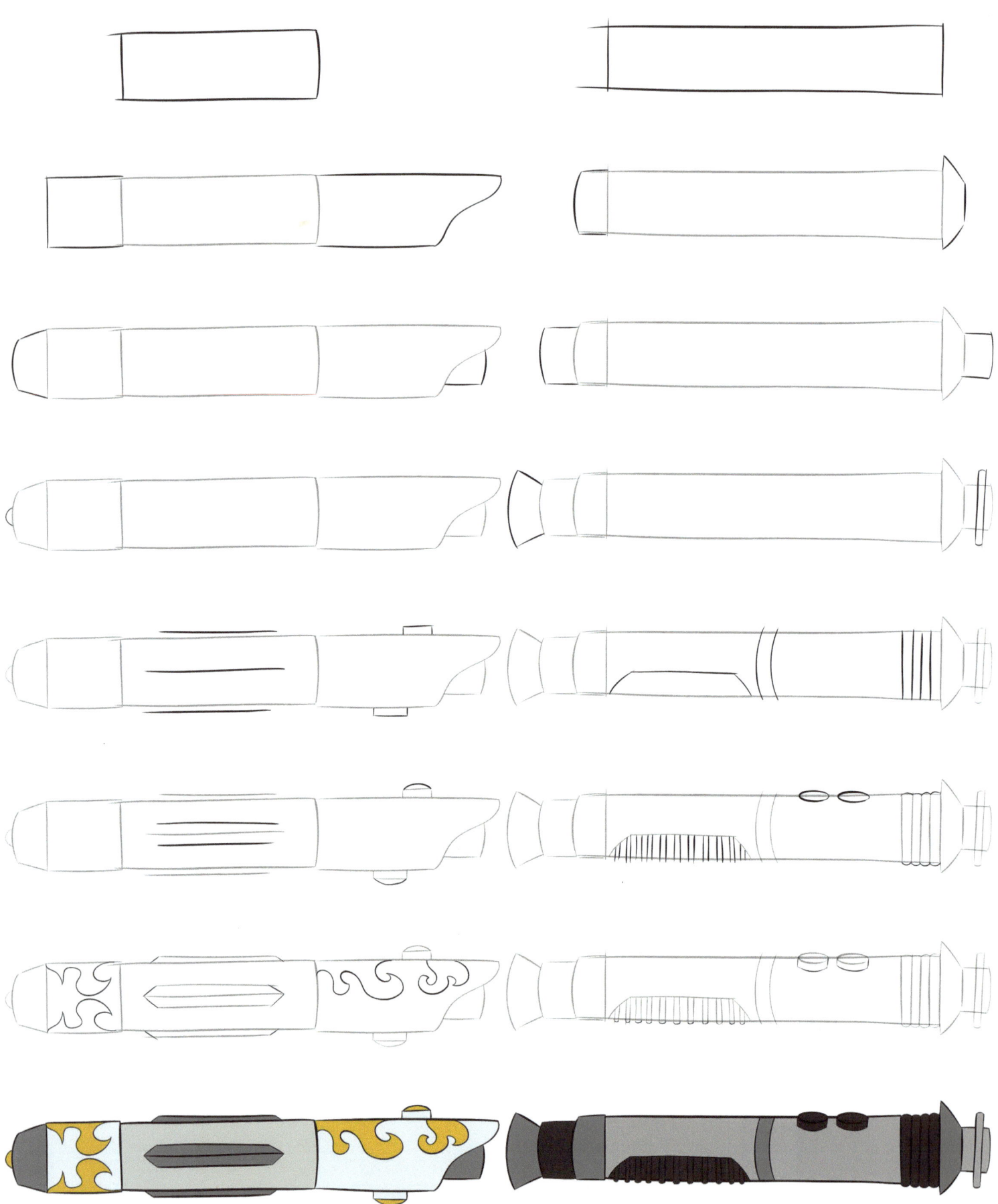

# Remember:
# Drawing is about having fun!

Don't worry about making the perfect circle or square, just keep practicing. Don't draw just what is in this book, take what you've learned and create your own creatures and characters.

For other books and tutorials please visit

www.shawndurington.com

or

www.facebook.com/ArtofShawnDurington

Join us in our drawing group on Facebook:
Drawing with Melvin and Me